for the Boulton family,
from
~~~~~~~~~~~

Christmas 199_

Other People's Children

By the same author

Vernon Phillips Watkins, The Early Years

Table of Contents

Chapters

List of illustrations

Frontispiece: The author and friend, Compton Martin, 1939.

Centrefold: A selection of photographs from the author's album.

Chapter 1
Early days

I suppose it all began in the imposing Parish Church in the Mumbles, Gower, which we attended as a family in the early 1920's. Being very young, the religious services did not impress me at all, but I watched intently for the arrival of the children from the Diocesan Orphanage, Thistleboon, and then hardly took my eyes off them from first to last. There were about thirty in number, mostly girls of all ages, with only a scattering of little boys. The girls wore scarlet cloaks over their grey uniforms, which seemed to lighten up the grey pillars and sombre pews of the old church. Seeing my curiosity, my mother explained the purpose of an or-phanage and the sad fact that these children had lost their parents.

My immediate reaction was not of sympathy but to marvel at the romantic implications of being an orphan. Why, without parents, one could be simply anyone! The possi-bilities were endless, and my lively imagination filled the orphanage with fantasy and adventure far removed from the actual hard work and plain living experienced by the inmates.

Life within my own affectionate family was a singularly happy one. It never occurred to me to compare my lot with that of an orphan, who I imbued with fairytale unreality. From time to time my parents took me to Thistleboon to visit the children with small presents of sweets and toys, and in time I became more aware of what it meant to be an orphan, or, at any rate, a child apart from its parents. When I was old enough to do so I arranged with a friend to take the children out for walks on Saturdays, or to play indoor games with them when it was wet. One of the most popular was a very old-fashioned singing game with the rather lugubrious refrain:

1

"Wallflowers, wallflowers, growing up so high,
We are little children and we shall all die..."

This was sung with great zest, and no one seem dismayed
by its message.

Thistleboon Orphanage was run by Miss Scott, a large,
imposing lady, who was stone deaf and carried a huge ear
trumpet. All the children would curtsey before speaking
into this rather alarming contraption, the smallest would
have to climb onto a chair in order to do so. They did this
without fear, though always addressing Miss Scott as 'Lady',
a title she thoroughly deserved after a lifetime of love and
devotion to the children in her care. Her assistant, Miss
Mossop, was as small as her superior was large, and scurried
round the house like a faithful sheep dog. She, in turn, was
assisted by one, sometimes two, of the girls who had grown
up in the Home but remained on to care for the younger
ones. The old-fashioned atmosphere was cheerful and contented.

I was lucky enough to grow up in a splendid Victorian
house in Caswell Bay, only a few miles from the orphanage.
It was a marvelous place for children, with lots of room and
a big garden running down to the bay. My mother shared
my interest in Thistleboon, and before long we had arranged with Miss Scott to invite the children to tea with us
on their birthdays. Though they must always have lived
with a sense of loss, most seemed a happy lot. No doubt
some were not, and I remember one very pretty gipsy girl
named Nan, with a club foot, who chose always to rebel. In
later years it was darkly whispered that she 'had come to a
bad end', not, as Dylan Thomas would have said "very
agreeable".

At the time there was no thought that my visits to
Thistleboon would begin to create a lifelong interest in
other people's children, and primarily in those deprived of
ordinary home lives.

Chapter 2
The first adventure

After the first World War, work opportunities for untrained middle-class girls were scarce indeed. Apart from a public school education and fairly fluent French (I had spent my eighteenth year in France), I had little to offer a less than interested world, except good health, energy and a cheerful disposition. Though an avid reader I was not an intellectual as my brother and sister were. My mind was probably sharpened by the constant interchange of ideas in our stimulating family life, but the glories of an unspoiled Gower, where the sea ebbed and flowed at our doorstep, lay around us and called me equally to the out-of-doors. It was only the dominant need of the young for independence which ultimately drove me out into the working world, immature, idealistic and romantic.

Unknown to my parents I found my first job through an advertisement in the 'Personal' column of *The Times*. It asked for an au pair girl to teach English and supervise outdoor activities in a small school for maladjusted children of fifteen different nationalities, on the shores of Lac Leman near Geneva. The Principal, a young Danish woman, told me later that she had chosen me from over 70 applicants because of my handwriting. Since this had always been ridiculed by my family as incredibly bad, I was rather amazed.

The school was housed in a large villa, the grounds ran right down to the edge of the lake, and there were glorious views of the mountains and a distant glimpse of Geneva. Of the three dozen pupils, most were girls of all ages, with a few boys aged from eight to fourteen. Six of the girls were teenaged Scandinavians, there to perfect their French, and also to learn a little English from their young and inexperienced teacher.

Though all of the younger children showed varying degrees of maladjustment, by far the worst were the Corsican

3

twins, Jean Jerome and Charles, aged nine, who seemed to combine all the most abominable traits of their illustrious countryman. The twins were the offspring of a blind Corsican Army officer and his American wife, and certainly top the long list of the really difficult children I have ever known. They quarrelled incessantly, both with each other and everyone else. When cornered neither would hesitate to use a knife; if defeat seemed inevitable, one or both would escape to the garden and shin up the nearest tree. Anyone unwise enough to attempt to dislodge them might be showered with pee from above. They served me, however, better than they knew. In later life when I was confronted by gross misbehaviour with problem children, the memory of the Corsican twins gave me strength and patience. Current misdeeds paled into insignificance by comparison, and therefore were placed in a hopeful perspective.

The school's Principal, Madame Kullman, was a gifted teacher and young enough to tolerate running a mixed regime of demanding children from so many different cultures. I suspected that some pupils were dumped there because their parents could not control them, and did not want the trouble of dealing with readjustments. Her assistant in the school was her exact opposite. A small, mouselike woman, she amused me one day when the children were being particularly obstreperous by remarking in a low voice, "*Mademoiselle, avec ces enfants il faut etre un tigre.*" No one could have been less like one.

My English classes were largely conversational and I, for one, actively enjoyed them. As the fine spring days approached, Madame Kullman would suddenly decide that the weather was too good to waste indoors, and the whole school would abandon learning and prepare for a picnic in the mountains. We never reached the snow, but I loved these easy climbs where we followed Madame in single file as if she were a female Pied Piper. The return home would be when the distant heights above us were turning from white to a soft rose colour as the sun lit the snow.

4

Though I had enjoyed working with these children, and was even undaunted by the terrible twins, my post at the school was unpaid. After some months I decided that I must begin to earn some money so I returned home resolved to look again for work with children, this time on a paid basis.

In spite of her Oxford degree, my sister Marjorie was also unemployed. We agreed to spend a week together in London looking for work. We decided to be governesses, on the grounds that what was good enough for the Bronte sisters previously should be good enough for us now. Sharing a room in Gower Street for only 30/- a week, we were soon doing the rounds of agencies in our search for employment. Marjorie quickly found a teaching post in Gloucestershire, in charge of a group of children who attended private classes in a large house.

I was offered an interview with a Countess who was looking for a governess for her two little girls of seven and nine. Believing that this was within my compass, I was engaged immediately to start work for the princely sum of 50 pounds a year, all found.

Chapter 3
Another world

The Earl and Countess lived on an estate in the heart of rural England, where the drives were over a mile long and the nearest town ten miles away. The vast park had contained deer, no doubt killed off centuries ago, as hunting was the main passion of the family. A pack of hounds bayed away in their own palatial quarters. The horses, too, lived like lords. Rather better, I think, than the one who employed me.

The old Earl had died some years previously. Since his demise the establishment of twenty-four indoor servants and twelve gardeners had been halved, while the single bathroom had been increased to nine. The old Earl never tolerated the idea of using any bath but his own, a tin one, and that article accompanied him on his travels.

When I arrived to start work I found that the children's quarters in the west wing comprised one very large bedroom which I was to share with my two charges. The only privacy afforded was by two large screens around my bed. This I found hard because, even at boarding school and certainly in my own home, I always had a room of my own.

The equally large schoolroom was next door and chiefly occupied by two full-size kitchen tables entirely covered with miniature farm buildings and animals of every description. Simple to see where the children's interests lay! As soon as I met Lady Anne and Lady Joan I was provided with paper and pencil and asked to draw a horse. Sensing the vital importance of making sure that the animal came up to scratch, I was more than relieved when my painful efforts passed muster.

Both children were shy but friendly and I liked them immediately. Soon after the 'horse trial' I was led to a much smaller room on the same floor to meet the youngest member of the family, a one year old girl, and her Nannie. Here I found the reason for the older children's faint cockney accents. Nannie had been responsible for the upbringing of all three from birth. She was a remarkable person, and was to become the only close adult friend I made while there. Protocol declared that governesses and nannies should live apart. This seemed absolute nonsense to me, and I believe we both gained from our companion-ship.

My first installation was a radio in the nursery, and in return Nannie taught me how to knit. She regaled us with stories of other children in the great houses where she had worked. On fine days she sometimes allowed me to push the baby in her splendid pram when we were all out together. Riding was my pupils' absorbing interest and one which I shared with them. Most fortunate this was, as apart from walking in the grounds there was nothing else to do. I had brought my bicycle with me and soon persuaded my employers to buy Anne and Joan one each. Overall I was secretly appalled by the restricted lives they led in such marked contrast to my own lively childhood experience.

The girls had minimal contact with their parents. Apart from a short visit at breakfast, and an hour or so after tea, when Anne and Joan put on party clothes complete with bronze dancing slippers for the occasion, we lived separate lives. All our meals were served to us in the schoolroom. Not surprisingly these were never hot, as the unfortunate parlour maid had what seemed to me a day's march to carry them from the kitchen.

On Sundays we attended the charming little church in the park, where the Earl read the lessons, surrounded by effigies and reminders of the past. This was followed by lunch in the large dining room, the only meal in the week I enjoyed in the house outside the schoolroom. Conversation rarely strayed beyond local or county interests. I sadly missed the cut and thrust of our talk at home, where no subject was banned and poetry, politics and sport came in for lively discussion.

It was not that the children were dull, simply that their interests and experience were severely limited. Anne had an excellent brain and was a good learner. She had a sweet nature but her terrible shyness made communication difficult. Joan, unlike her sister, had real learning difficulties. She also had a slightly crippled arm following an accident in infancy. Despite these handicaps, Joan was a most attractive, affectionate child, with a rather gruff voice which I found most endearing.

The two played endlessly with their individual farm toys which were far more interesting than other playthings. It was amusing to find that all their dolls had titles, not an indication of snobbishness, but simply because titles were the norm in the household. Though I do not recall any great parental interest in the girls' education, the Countess and Earl were kind and co-operative over any suggestions I made to them. One idea I presented was to start a Guide company in the nearest village, largely so that ten year old Anne could join it. She soon was able to enjoy her first entry into normal village life.

For me the interest of this work was to be able to observe the phenomena of the different world around me. I knew that I was free to leave it when I wished and this knowledge made the job tolerable. I decided to stay there for a year, and to do my very best for the children in the meantime.

An amusing aspect of my life there was the snobbery of the servants' hall. The butler and cook ruled the roost, and though in repute a governess was usually despised by the fraternity as being neither fish nor fowl, I seemed to be well-accepted by everyone. My lack of ceremony must have disturbed the rather pompous butler. When I persuaded him to help me move furniture or toys, he would say "This is not a butler's work, Miss", but would do it all the same.

A highlight of the year was the month when Anne, Joan and I visited the beautiful home of their grandmother. Not unduly large, with velvet lawns surrounded by yew hedges, I think it was the most perfect house in which I have ever stayed. Being a hot summer, I imagined earlier days when the Earl and his brother had played cricket on the lawn with the butler and the footman.

The grandmother, a woman of charm and repose, spent most of her days reclining on a sofa by a large log fire. She was always surrounded by her pekinese dogs, which I found a definite hazard to my feet. On fine days the Viscountess would emerge as far as the rose garden, where she would languidly dead-head the faded blooms. This seemed to be her ultimate exertion, though I should add that she was far from young. My energy and youth must have sometimes appalled her, and though I was always treated most kindly, occasionally I caught her looking at me as if I were a strange animal with dangerous potential.

A clear memory is the dining room with its high shelf encircling it, on which sat pairs of china dogs of every size and description, giving the room a unique charm. The food was excellent, as a French chef was lord of the staff. He lived with his tame jackdaw in a cottage in the grounds, and I heard later that he had been sacked for extravagance when he used twenty-four eggs in a souffle. A sad loss, I thought.

Best of all, I was allowed the freedom of the library, where, among other delights, I found the complete works of Samuel Pepys. These I read, whenever I was free to do so, for the whole month of our stay. My own extensive letter writing soon bore signs of the Master: 'Rose betimes, etc.' I would begin my correspondence, but alas, could never keep it up in the same vein.

When my year was up, I gave the Countess a month's notice. Expressing regret, she said that she had hoped I would have remained on to complete the girls' education. I was tempted to ask her bluntly whether the restricted life offered here was likely to challenge any reasonably intelligent young teacher or governess. In fact, I replied that Anne deserved a far better education than I could give her. I might have added that Joan needed more skilled and supportive help.

We parted on good terms. I was sorry to leave the children and Nannie, but otherwise regarded the episode as a venture into a world far removed from my own, one which would never again be my choice. Years later I met Nannie in London. She had retired and was living with her sister. The Countess had given her notice to quit as soon as all the children had out-grown the nursery. When I remarked on the hardness of this after so many years of devoted service, she replied without rancour that her ladyship was not sentimental. All the same I think there should at least have been an additional record in the family church to mark that woman's long years as substitute mother.

Chapter 4
To Ireland and Hungary

After a glorious holiday at home in Gower, and armed with a good reference, I decided to look for work abroad. I soon found it with an Irish lady then living in Dinard, Brittany, who wanted a governess for her six year old twins, Dominic and Marcia. The only tiresome proviso was that I should speak French at all times to the children. Although my French was fluent, I found it tedious trying to teach in that language, and subsequently so did the children.

Dominic was a wizened, cross-eyed little boy, with pronounced learning difficulties, and hopelessly poor physical co-ordination. He had quite enough to contend with, even in his own language. In spite of his oddities, he was much more likeable than his complacent sister, Marcia, who appeared to delight in her twin's shortcomings, and did nothing to help him. We lived as a family and it was a joy being in Brittany again, where I had spent several holidays as a child. The swimming was a pleasure and altogether life was smooth and undemanding.

When the twins' mother announced that she would be moving with the children back to Ireland, I was glad to go with them. I had never been to Ireland though both my brother, Vernon, and I were then deeply enthralled in Anglo-Irish literature. W.B. Yeats was the idol of the hour, so I was delighted to hear that we were to spend the following summer in County Mayo, not far from his old haunts.

I shall never forget my first glimpse of Rosturk Castle, a mock Gothic edifice on the edge of Clew Bay, where we were to stay. As we rounded the coast on arrival, this magical spot exceeded all my romantic expectations. Clew Bay is dotted with countless small islands and at low tide the black cattle wade through shallow water from the mainland to graze on the island which lay opposite Rosturk.

Mercifully it was a fine summer, and I never tired of watching the changing panorama of light and shade on land and water, with only the cries of the curlew and munching cattle to disturb the peace.

Staying with us in Rosturk Castle were Mrs. Waldron, the twins' grandmother, and her farouche daughter, Noel, whose whole life seemed to have been spent with horses. We all lived together as family and apart from the appalling chore of trying to speak French non-stop to two apparently deaf children, everything in the castle was lovely.

Mrs. Waldron was a highly cultivated woman of distinction and elegance, in absolute contrast to Noel, whose manners reeked of the stable. I still remember the occasion at one meal, when Noel's bad manners provoked her mother to say very gently, "Really, Noel dear, I think you have lived too much alone......"

I have only the haziest memories of teaching the two small children, though I recall vividly the hours I spent prawning in the bay, or collecting fresh cockles which the cook would convert expertly into a mock-oyster soup. Sometimes with a favourite poetry book, I would climb the hills which lay behind the castle, until it was time to return to duties which consisted mainly of protecting Dominic from his smug sister.

During that summer I first visited Achill Island, which quickly took next place to Gower in my affections. Sixty years ago the island's population could be measured in hundreds, its marvelous beaches topped by sheer cliffs were largely deserted. Fishing was the islanders main occupation and their long, black curraghs seemed able to cut through the wildest seas. Even when the water was reasonably calm, to embark on a trip in one was like riding in an old Ford car on a very rough road. The people of Achill had all the charm and simplicity so common in the west of Ireland, before cars, television and tourism cast their corrupting spells.

I shall always be grateful to this Irish family for the memorable introduction to County Mayo that they made possible for me. Alas! at the end of the summer the family moved to a dull house in a remote part of southern Ireland. I had been so intoxicated by County Mayo that it was simply impossible for me to accept the change. Rather ungratefully I left the job and returned to Gower. At this time, I fear I was far more concerned with what I got out of work than what I put into it, though trying to give good value to my employers and their children while I was in post.

*

My next venture was to join the family of a diplomat attached to the British Legation in Budapest, to look after nine year old Diana, the only child in this quite delightful family. In appearance the diplomat looked a typical Blimp, by no means the smooth person I had expected. His service in the Black Watch as a regular officer had ended after the first World War, and he had then joined the Diplomatic Service.

Travelling to Budapest from London with Diana and her mother, we were met on night arrival at the station with the deafening roar of "Hullo, old cock!" from a large, red-faced man to his delighted daughter, who was quickly smothered in an equally exuberant hug. If I were ever to write a book on the 'Best father I have known', this diplomat would top the list.

The more I came to know this man the more I liked him. With a total lack of pomp, he combined high intelligence and total integrity with an overpowering sense of humour. He adored his wife and Diana and seemed oblivious to the prissy conventions of the diplomatic life around him. Typically, he learned to speak fluent Hungarian from his chauffeur, and was, I think, one of very few Englishmen to pass the diplomatic examination in that difficult language. His wife shared his intelligence but not his unconventionality, though her own sense of humour helped her to accept this.

Diana was a bright, affectionate child, both nervous and highly sensitive, who lived in an imaginative fantasy world. Her father regaled her with endless tales of the exploits of two characters he had invented, called Scouty and Guidy, and his letters to the child were the most entertaining I have read. They could have been printed and published for other children to enjoy. Diana was companionable in return and easy to teach. Soon she shared my love of poetry and when lessons were over, Budapest had many other occupations to offer.

Sometimes we bathed in the most advanced swimming pool in Buda. Artificial waves were produced, always preceded by a tiny man tooting on a horn. This warning alerted the more nervous swimmers that they could escape the waves if they would just be quick. As the weather changed and got colder, we would drive down the Andrazy Utza - the longest main street in Europe, I was told - to the moated castle at the end. A conversion had produced an ice rink there upon which we all had glorious fun, even though neither of us was a good skater. The family always included me in their evening parties, and there were some fascinating people to meet. On one red letter occasion the great ballerina, Karsavina and her handsome English husband came to dinner. He was then an adviser to the Bank of Hungary, having been forced to leave the Diplomatic Service when he married a dancer. Karsavina combined grace and charm with a natural dignity which was most impressive.

Diana's mother, Mrs. X, was an excellent bridge player and would sometimes arrange evening bridge parties. On these occasions I would usually join her husband - who had no interest in the game whatsoever - at what I can only describe as a nursery table, with others who were deemed to be on an equally low level of skill. Nationalities were always mixed and play would proceed in Hungarian, French and sometimes Polish. I was the better player than the diplomat, but his hilarious asides in English usually made serious bridge impossible.

14

Hungarian is really an impossible language to master while living in an English community, and I never learned to speak more than a few words. My inability did not prevent me from exploring the beautiful city, but not without occasional hiccups. On one occasion when I had boldly boarded a tram to go further afield, a sudden sense of panic overcame me when I realised that the conductor would ask my destination. I had the wit to listen carefully to what my neighbour said, and when my turn came I gave the conductor a coin and made a noise more like a sneeze than anything else. The ticket was issued without further comment, and I left the tram when my neighbour got out. I must have found my way home, but I never had the temerity to use public transport on my own again.

Budapest was a city of enormous charm for me. In the early 1930's Admiral Horty was still Regent. The impression of life there amongst the rich and poor alike was almost feudal in structure. The excellent indoor servants would kiss the hem of the mistress' long evening dress before retiring for the night. Outside in that cold winter at least two young men died while sleeping rough. The old palaces in Buda were flood-lit and bracelets of light swung over the five bridges across the Danube where the rest of the city also was ablaze with light. The effect was magical.

One day we all went to the outskirts of the city to see the anniversary celebrations of the battle of the Field of Blood. I have no idea which of the many Balkan wars this commemorated but it was my first realisation of the hotch-potch of national hatreds and aspirations which steamed in this part of the world. As I watched regiments of Hungarian soldiers march through the mud, some wheeling their bicycles, they seemed to offer no threat to anyone. But I somehow sensed that this was the end of an era. Mingling in the crowds around us were a number of men in court dress, most of which was worn and shabby. They were like an old pack of cards, soon to be discarded for ever.

15

In December of that year the diplomat was recalled to London, and we left Budapest as the snow was beginning to fall. Everything glittered in the frost and as the train left the station I saw for the last time the brilliant lights of the city reflected in the waters of the Danube. I was sorry to say goodbye.

Back in London the family found a house to rent and Diana was able to attend an excellent day school. It was clear that I was no longer needed though her parents pressed me to remain on as a companion to the child. This was not at all my idea of life, however, so it was time to pack my bags and say farewell. We remained excellent friends over many years and Diana spent more than one holiday with me in Gower. But, for now, it was back to Gower for my usual long holiday with my own family before sallying forth again.

*

A family in Northern Ireland who lived near the Mourne mountains offered me the job of teaching their two small children, a boy and a girl. Part of the attraction was that I would be non-resident, could arrange my own lodgings and then teach and look after the children on a daily basis. Though I could not know it at the time, these people were to become life-long friends. Both parents have since died, but the children are still in touch, even though my little boy is now a grandfather.

The family home was delightful, well outside a seaside town and perched on a small hill within a glorious garden. It was not too large for comfort, and within view were the Mourne mountains where the children and I often climbed. Horses and hunting were the family's predominant interest, but unlike my first employers, both parents had far wider tastes. They abounded in kindness, generosity and humour, which combined with their endless hospitality made the atmosphere in their home warm and friendly.

16

Living in Newcastle lodgings was dreary, but I soon found a splendid converted bus to rent, on the edge of the golf links right on the sea shore. Though fairly primitive, it suited me and there was a farm nearby from which two little boys would stagger over with a large bucket of water when I gave them a shout.

I was always invited to join in the family holidays and these were wonderful. One summer we stayed in Connemara at the Renvyle Hotel (the former home of Oliver St. John Gogarty) with all the delights of County Mayo and Achill Island at hand. Another holiday was spent at Portmeirion, North Wales, which had just been opened as a hotel by the outstanding architect, Clough Williams Ellis. Inspired by an Italian seaside village, only the perpetual rain failed to complete the idyll. Even so, we were able to bathe in all weathers in magnificent scenery and 'fun' was the rule.

Chapter 5
Youth work in East London

My sister, Marjorie, had by this time exchanged teaching for social work. Her first post was with the Invalid Children's Aid Association, in a branch in Bethnal Green where she was to spend the rest of her working life. Like many other social workers in that lively district, she lived at St. Margaret's House Settlement in Victoria Park, and maintained a close link with the Settlement until her retirement in 1967.

I was, at last, growing up. Although I could never hope to find more congenial employers and surroundings than those in Northern Ireland, and I loved the company of children, continually finding new interest in them, my capacities as a teacher were very limited. French and English Literature were my only good subjects, and any sort of routine I found excessively boring. So, once again, farewells were said with friendliest feelings on all sides. A bit reluctantly I left the glorious scenery of County Down for the grimier surroundings of East London. Early in 1936, with Marjorie's help, I was appointed as an Assistant Club Leader on what was then the Marquis of Northampton's Estate in Islington.

The club premises were in a large house at the top of St. John's Street, near the Angel, where the Club Leader, another Dorothy (Fox), and I lived on the first floor. The clubs were provided for the Estate's tenants and served all ages, from young to old. Miss Fox and I were the only paid helpers, though there were a number of excellent volunteers, some of whom provided 'keep fit' and dancing classes for the younger members. It was a fascinating introduction to life in East London, and though living in a city did not suit me at all, as a Dickens fan I recognised Goswell Road and found that quite a few Artful Dodgers were still around. Endless entertainment was provided by being within easy reach of the river, the whole of the City and the St. Paul's area, while the Bethnal Green Road led off to Marjorie's settlement. Nonetheless I could not look as I walked along it, at the live eel stall with its unhappy, writhing occupants.

Apart from the club work, I was also attached to the Care Committee of the local London County Council School. This involved visiting homes in the area to sort out various problems with parents related to their children's attendance. One rather dreary home I visited in St. John's Street to discuss the poor school attendance of a small girl with her rather dim mother, went quite according to form, until I asked innocently about the baby lying quietly in a cradle in the corner of the room, "Oh," said the crestfallen mother, "that's my little misfortune." As there seemed to be no supporting male in the picture, this may have been only too true a description. The club work usually began in the afternoon, sometimes with tea and chat for the local mothers' group, who were often accompanied by their small children. After school the older children would arrive, much less easily pleased and often quite unruly.

Fourteen was then the school-leaving age, and it shocked me to think these children had to start work when wealthier contemporaries were just beginning their public school education.

Games and dancing dominated the teen age clubs, but except for the occasional drunk, both sexes were equally friendly and amenable. Things did not always go smoothly, of course. A live cat was once flung onto the crowded dance floor from the street window. Luckily it came to no harm, no one was hurt and the dancing soon resumed. Nor was I meekly accepted by all, as an expertly flung tomato landing on my left ear demonstrated.

One volunteer was a trained dancing instructor and she offered to run a ballet class for girls from five to eight in age. Not to be completely outshone I made the pants and tunics for the dancers from a bale of check gingham. Lo and behold, by the time the first class was to start, there was a crowd of cherubic would-be ballerinas. Sometimes, when

19

the clubs closed early, I hurried off to see the ballet, then close by in the Sadlers Wells premises, where, at half time I was admitted for 6d standing.

The Christmas Tenants' Tea for 800 children was a memorable occasion. Miss Fox, surveying the heavily-laden tables in the enormous hall before the swarming crowds entered, suddenly exclaimed with alarm. Lump and not granulated sugar had been put on the tea tables. Seeing my perplexity she explained that the previous year one child had suffered a cut eye when the lump sugar was successfully used as a missile. The change was quickly effected, and after a Light Brigade charge from the doorway, the party went uproariously well. No sour - or sweet - mishaps.

Summer club holidays were arranged for all ages. We took the Brownies to a camp near Hazelmere, and the Girl Guides camped in Lord Northampton's beautiful park at Castle Ashby. In each case it was the splendid trees which were such an attraction. Having spent nearly all my life until then in the country, I was not finding it easy to adapt to living in the City.

Marjorie and I would steal away to the nearest countryside whenever we were both free together. On one of these outings in Kent, we saw a notice perched in a tree saying 'Carnival for Sale'. This turned out to be a gipsy caravan, only the spelling had gone wrong. It was evening when we found the place and were invited to look inside by the gipsy owner. To our amusement four little heads popped out from the lower bunk. Our offer of 10 pounds was quickly accepted and the caravan was ours. We moved it onto land owned by a friendly girl who ran a nearby riding school. After an alarming but mercifully short battle against a legacy of bugs that the gipsies had left us, our country retreat was perfect.

One day, to our astonishment, a group of Cossacks went riding by. We learned that our hostess had also given sanctuary to a team of Cossacks and their horses after a riding display at Olympia. This place and its inhabitants were such a welcome antidote to London, and we all became great friends. Some time later we were delighted to learn that the most gorgeous of the Cossacks and the riding school mistress became man and wife.

The highlight of that glorious summer of 1937 was the bank holiday week in August when I took a lively group of club girls to camp at Whitstable. I shall never forget the girls' cries of alarm when confronted by the tents in which we were all to sleep. Somehow I managed to convince them that they would come to no harm, and the splendid weather helped to make the holiday a success. Never having been to Whitstable before, we were all fascinated by the great expanse of sea and shore, lit up in the evenings by spectacular sunsets.

Miss Fox, always full of enterprise, planned a coach trip for the over-18 year olds to Bruges for Easter, 1938. I offered to run French conversational classes during the preceding winter, and though I cannot claim to have produced fluent linguists, the classes were hilarious. I was never short of pupils among whom were pretty factory girls and stalwart young lorry drivers. One fellow shouted out from the back of the class, "What's the French for'give 'em the works'?" and that left me somewhat nonplussed as to how the trip would turn out. The young people saved up all winter for this spree, and we stayed in a modest pension in Bruges. My major responsibilities were to act as interpreter between our Cockney contingent and the French girls and boys they soon met, and to see that none of our lot was left behind on coach outings. I was amazed at how well everyone behaved on the trip. I little guessed that the following year would see a number of them back in Europe in the armed forces.

The day outing of the Mothers' Club to Margate that summer was an altogether more uproarious affair. By coach we rollicked from one pub to another on our way to the ocean. After a bit of paddling and jellied eels all round at Margate, it was time to start for home, and the mums were in excellent form. A spirited rendering of 'Knees up Mother

Brown' in song and dance at the final pub completed the outing, and it would probably be more than a year before they even contemplated another.

At the time of the Munich conference in 1938, a World War seemed all too probable, and some of the younger club girls began to work themselves up to an almost hysterical state. In trying to induce a more sensible attitude, I was brought up short by one fourteen-year old girl who commented sharply, "It's alright for you, Miss, you've had your life." I was 28 at the time.

In East London I learned a great deal, and grew to like and admire the cheerful spunk so often to be found in the born Cockney. Living conditions on the Northampton Estate were by no means easy, and most of the families I met were poor. I suspect that the old habits of stealing which Dickens portrayed in Goswell Road had not entirely disappeared. There were dark murmurs of razor gangs among the Italians in Soho not far away, but I do not recall other nationalities among the Estate's tenants. Although there were numerous jokes about 'nicking' in the clubs, there was never any bad language in my presence. Looking back, it seems by modern day standards to have been a rather innocent way of life.

One evening I went to a hall in London to hear a speaker on child migration, and the work of a voluntary society called The Fairbridge Farm Schools. The scheme allowed deprived children in depressed areas of British cities to emigrate to Australia where they would be cared for in farm school communities. My interest was immediate due to my strong inclination for country life as opposed to that of the city. I supported the idea of giving under-privileged children a chance of a better life overseas. Having seen enough poverty and frustration in the over-crowded conditions of East London the idea of wide open spaces, was welcome, and especially in a continent where a poor start need not be a lasting disadvantage. I believed, and still do, that almost anyone benefits from growing up in the country.

It was not long before I visited the Director of The Fairbridge Society, at Savoy House in the Strand. Gordon Green was an ebullient Australian and his assistant, Ellen Hart, along with their efficient secretary, Dorothy Hall, made up the London headquarters staff. These three were dynamic and dedicated, and I was most impressed by the friendly atmosphere in the Fairbridge office as well as the staff's enthusiastic concern for the children they were trying to help.

The Society had been started by Kingsley Fairbridge before the first World War. He had come to Oxford from South Africa as a Rhodes Scholar, the poor and over-crowded conditions in the inner cities appalled him, particularly the way in which so many deprived children were struggling to survive. The British Empire was still, of course, a flourishing concern at the time. When Kingsley Fairbridge with the help of others took a group of destitute children from Britain to found the first Farm School in Western Australia, the scheme was wide applauded and supported. Fairbridge himself died young, but the work of the Society grew, until by 1937 there were three Farm Schools in Australia and one in Canada.

The emotional effects of uprooting a child from however inadequate a home were little appreciated before the last war. I certainly did not understand them at the time. It seemed to me vital to select only those children who were extrovert and fairly tough, so that they would be likely to fit into a large rural community. With my own passion for travel and new experiences, it surprised no one when I offered to act as a voluntary escort to a party of emigrant children should an opportunity arise. Meantime I went on with the club work which I really enjoyed.

World affairs became increasingly sombre. On a walk by the Thames Embankment in the summer of 1938 I saw two machine guns being placed there, only a small indication of what was to come. Early in 1939 I received an SOS from Gordon Green asking me to stand by to take a party of eighteen children in a month's time to Australia. Without hesitation I gave in my notice to poor Miss Fox. She was not too dismayed as it was normal practice for young assistants to move on to other jobs after a couple of years invaluable experience in club work.

By chance, while awaiting final orders from Fairbridge, there was a small crisis at St. Margaret's House, where Marjorie worked. Both the fully employed Club leaders had fallen ill and there was no one at all to take charge of their thriving clubs. I knew the warden, Miss Kelly, and some of the twenty-four residents well due to my frequent visits by bicycle from the Angel to Bethnal Green. Although I had always teased them about living in what I called Austerity Hall, nicknaming the residents 'the pussies', I genuinely liked the place. In no time I found myself acting as its temporary Youth Club Leader -- for about six weeks, until the crisis was over.

Chapter 6
Child Migration -- Australia

We were to sail in March 1939. With a little money I had saved, added to the travelling expenses which the Fairbridge Society were providing, I was soon ready to be off.

I went up to London a couple of days earlier to attend a farewell party for the emigrant children at Australia House. This was my first encounter with the lively bunch of boys and girls that I was to take to Australia. Their ages ranged from five to thirteen, only three were girls.

The contrast between these excited and irrepressible children and their august hosts was very diverting. After they had devoured an enormous tea, a slightly pompous big wig made a speech all about the glories of the Empire. The poor man suffered little short of heckling, as questions were shot at him by the children as well as frequent demands by the younger members to leave the room.

That same night the children and I stayed in a Fairbridge hostel at Holland Park. Few got much sleep, but there were certainly no tears when we entrained to Liverpool to join the SS Esperance Bay. The ship was one-class, and part of the Aberdeen and Commonwealth Line. As the ship was crowded with emigrants of all ages, I was pleased to be met by the other two escorts who were to help me on the voyage. The man, Mr. Birdseye, was planning to settle in Australia himself, and the girl was going out to a nursing post.

Some emigrants were sponsored by the Salvation Army, others, mostly Jewish, had left Germany for obvious reasons to make a new life overseas. I could not help thinking what a marvelous contribution these intelligent people were likely to make in the country of their adoption.

Meanwhile we bustled round to get the children settled into their various cabins while I also kept a strict eye on the fifty-two cases which contained their new outfits, as well as games and simple text books for occupation on board. The children were far too excited to be home-sick. Some had come direct from Children's Homes, others were from one-parent families. All were delighted with the ship. At our first meal in the dining saloon, Bernard, aged seven, attacked his soup with a fork until I advised him that he would do better with a spoon. I doubt whether any of the children had seen such a choice of cutlery before.

In a large ship it was difficult to prevent them from scattering all over the place, and naturally getting into mischief. When one of the sailors reported to me laconically that two of my boys had climbed twenty feet up the rigging, I felt it was time to draw a firm line. All climbing was strictly forbidden, and remarkably soon we established an effective routine. Simple lessons and games occupied most of the morning, and as soon as the weather warmed, the swimming pool was in constant use. The adult passengers were friendly and tolerant, and all the crew were delightful with the children.

Mr. Birdseye seemed most at home with our three little girls, and I soon saw that he really could not control the boys at all. The other escort, whose name I cannot even remember, caught German Measles at the beginning of the trip and was in quarantine for nearly the whole of the five week voyage.

Luckily I greatly enjoyed the boys' company, and Joey, aged five, became my inseparable companion. He was one of a family of four, and like many of the others, came from the Tyneside, having all the charm and independence so often found in people from that hard-pressed area. Joey was not a beauty, nor were his brother and sisters, but what they lacked in looks they made up for in personality. I was told that when all the children were examined by the Immigration authorities to check their suitability, Henry, Joey's elder brother, marched in saying that it was no good taking children in ones and twos, a family of four was much better together, and should, of course, be selected. As they were all rather undersized and inclined to be bandy, I can only surmise that it was Henry's cheek that got them through. One day when Joey was missing I found him in the dining saloon, where solemnly he told me he was helping the steward to polish the seats.

Once every week I unlocked the children's suitcases to give them a change of clean clothes. Even in the stifling heat when we reached the Red Sea there was never a shortage of volunteers to help me with the washing and ironing. Two or three of the older boys, clad only in bathing trunks, would descend with me to the laundry below deck and cheerfully set to work. A more willing set of workers could never be found.

By the time we reached Melbourne, where all but one of the children were to disembark for the Northcott Farm School in Victoria, I would gladly have taken the whole lot to the ends of the earth, in fact the idea of leaving them in strange hands was quite painful.

It was getting dark when we finally docked in Melbourne, and Joey asked me whether it was always night in Australia, thinking, no doubt, that as we were now on the other side of the world, this might well be so.

We soon piled into a coach and were off to the Farm School a few miles away. I was fascinated to see parrots on the telegraph wires, instead of our more mundane starlings. We were given a rousing reception by all the staff and children on arrival, and there were some touching reunions among the newly arrived and their elder brothers and sisters already at home on the Farm. The first thing our young emigrants did was to pull off their shoes and socks, though their tender feet could not cope with the sun-baked earth as well as their hardy, bare-footed companions.

I had dreaded a tearful parting from Joey, but quickly absorbed into the new environment, he left me without a qualm. I rejoined the ship with David, aged thirteen, with whom I was to travel on to the Fairbridge Farm School at Molong, New South Wales. We sailed to Sydney, which was a great experience for us both, then there was an eight-hour train journey to the nearest station to the Farm School where we were met and given an equally friendly reception on our arrival. I was invited to remain as a guest until the time came for me to return to Sydney to catch the Esperance Bay on her homeward journey.

The community was set in a totally rural area in pleasant surroundings which combined mixed farming with orchards and, I believe, some vineyards. The weather was brilliant by day and cold at night. I missed the sea as I had never stayed so far away from it.

The two hundred and fifty boys and girls were housed in cottages, with sixteen in each in the care of a housemother on the Fairbridge Farm, on which every child over twelve was expected to do some work. They all attended local schools according to age and ability. There was no domestic staff employed in the cottages, and all the children were expected to give their cottage mother a hand as required. This was in stark contrast to the Childrens' Homes in Britain I came to know so well later, where domestic staff did all the work and the children none.

What impressed me at once was the children's confident and friendly bearing. They all looked enormously fit, and I heard that the emigrants were expected to double their weight and height in two years at the Farm School. Looking at them, I could well believe it. The atmosphere generally was excellent. No doubt the children had hidden depths and sorrows beneath the surface, but during my month's stay I was not aware of them.

I was glad to be of any help I could and occasionally stood in for a cottage mother on her day off. Although very willing I viewed my new duties with some apprehension as I could not cook and had few domestic virtues.

Once when I was on duty I was invited to join some of the staff who were going by lorry to pick apples in an orchard some miles away. I was assured that we would be back long before the children returned from school, and so accepted with alacrity. All went well until the return journey when the wretched lorry broke down. This meant that my sixteen children would go without their tea, or be very late having it.

It was dark by the time I finally arrived back at the cottage, expecting to find at best some very cross, hungry children, at worst chaos. Instead, when I opened the door, I saw all the children sitting round the dining room table, having cooked and eaten their supper. " We have got yours in the oven," said the eldest boy kindly.

I think this brought home to me the vital importance of allowing children to feel of value, and that work well accomplished can play a great part in this.

When the time came for me to leave, Mr. and Mrs. Wood, the Principal and his wife, asked me to stay on at least for a time and I might well have done so, had the rumbles of approaching war not warned me that if I did not return home now it might be very difficult to do so later. Luckily for me, the Woods had to drive to Sydney and offered me a lift there when it was clear that I intended to catch the Esperance Bay. This gave me a marvellous chance to see more of Australia and I found the Blue Mountains very impressive, though secretly I thought the whole continent too big!

The Woods dropped me off near a large hotel in Sydney where I had no difficulty in getting a room. I arrived in the evening and was rather astonished to find the city full of drunken men. I had not realized it was Anzac Day when more drink is probably consumed in Australia than on any other day of the year.

I had a couple of days to explore the city and very much enjoyed strolling around the beautiful Botanical Gardens which seemed to stretch to the water's edge, and which I still remember as the best I have seen. The weather was wonderful and frequent ferries made it so easy to savour the delights of surfing on the nearby beaches. It was soon time to rejoin the Esperance Bay where I was given a great welcome by the Captain and crew.

When the ship called at Melbourne I was able to pay a final visit to the Northcott Farm School to see how my children had settled down. I was delighted to find them entirely absorbed in their new surrounding, in fact my dear Joey hardly stopped to say hullo.

I left feeling totally reassured of their well-being and rejoined the Esperance Bay very happily. We called at Tasmania to pick up a cargo of apples and I was able to climb Mount Wellington in perfect weather, with just time to gaze around that delightful island, before hurrying back to join the ship.

We arrived in England in June, by which time I almost felt I owned the Esperance Bay and was sorry to leave her. I had certainly had nothing but kindness on both the outward and return journeys.

Chapter 7
Compton Martin & Canada

Once more I was happy to spend a glorious summer of unemployment in Gower. My father had retired, and with my mother and only brother, had moved to a smaller house on the Pennard Cliffs about eight miles from Swansea. The position was marvellous, though it could never compete with Caswell Bay in my affections. I spent most of the summer in and around the sea, swimming off the rocks or surfing, and at low tide scrambling over the rocks with net and hook to search for prawns and lobsters.

Gordon Green had promised me a further trip as escort in the early autumn, this time to Vancouver Island where a Fairbridge Farm School had been established. An added bonus was that Dorothy Hall, on the Fairbridge London staff, was also to be an escort, and we planned a visit to the United States on the return journey as I, for one, had never been there.

Alas! we were due to sail on September 9th, 1939 and on the third I heard Chamberlain's sombre radio announcement that the country was at war. I remember strolling out on the peaceful Pennard Cliffs that evening and wondering what would become of us all.

I decided to volunteer for the Land Army, in the hope of being sent to North Wales where I could learn Welsh, as although both of my parents were Welsh-speaking none of their children had been brought up to speak it. It was not to be. I was told that as I was classified as a Social Worker I must look for work of this kind. While I was still pondering what to do, I had an urgent request from Gordon Green to go to Compton Martin in Somerset to look after the thirty boys and girls who had been evacuated there from the Fairbridge Hostel in London, pending emigration to Canada. I was assured that it would only be a few weeks before the necessary permit would be given us all to set sail for Vancouver.

I willingly packed my bags and set off by train for Somerset, not knowing the county well nor having any idea where I could stay in Compton Martin. No doubt my good angel guided me to the house of Irene and Charles Dawkins, in the centre of the village and conveniently opposite the Ring of Bells, the only pub in the place.

My brief from Fairbridge was to see that all the children who were scattered in various billets in Compton Martin, had adequate clothing and pocket money, and to sort out any difficulties that might arise. If possible I was also to rent a room where the children could meet out of school hours, for play and companionship. Fortunately, the Dawkins' house boasted a large front room which they allowed me to rent for this purpose. Their own two sons soon joined in the fun and it was not long before the playroom was crowded. As usual the majority of the Fairbridge children were boys, with a number of brothers and sisters among them.

There were, of course, some billeting problems. I once had an agitated, almost hysterical telephone call from a foster mother with whom three Fairbridge brothers were billeted, asking me to call round at once as something terrible had happened. Filled with foreboding I set off for the house at once, only to find that the smallest brother, a very fair child, had a head absolutely teeming with lice! The poor woman had never seen anything like it and stood staring at the creatures with stunned horror. A quick call to the chemist and vigorously applied shampoo did the trick and there was never anything more of that particular trouble.

I remained in close and friendly touch with the London Fairbridge staff, mostly by telephone and correspondence about the children's needs for clothing, etc., which were always quickly met.

As an instance of the splendid relationship between us all, their letters to me always started with the signs --. ? --

32

instead of my name, which was Dorothy Watkins (known to my friends as Dot) and were signed in the same way by me, in reply.

It soon became clear that we should remain in Compton Martin for the rest of the winter. I think we all enjoyed our stay there. I know I did.

I found the children enormously likeable, they were an older group, with several 'teen age boys, some of whom were very bright, and all were friendly and amusing.

As the days grew shorter the Dawkins' playroom would be crowded out with children after school; as well as games to play, I encouraged them to bring me any clothes that needed mending and I did my best to sew on buttons and generally patch them up.

The frosty nights were very dark and the main street of the village was a long one, so when the time came for bed, we would all muffle up well and arm-in-arm made our way up and down it, dropping the children off at their various billets. My attempts to draw their attention to the beauty of the night, with its brilliant stars and frost, were usually treated with derision but I like to think that some would remember their last, splendid winter in Somerset. The weather grew increasingly cold and by Christmas, Blagdon Lake had frozen over, and several other lakes and ponds provided splendid playgrounds for the children. Sometimes on Saturdays we would climb the Mendips to Priddy Pool. When the snow came it was an added joy.

On Christmas Eve Irene Dawkins and I filled a laundry basket with the children's presents, and delivered them to their billets under the light of a full moon, when the hillside trees were cracking under the weight of the snow, and the wayside grass stood up with spears of ice.

Fairbridge accepted children of all religious denominations, but the young Roman Catholic priest of a nearby village was the only Christian minister to show the smallest interest in the children. He was quick to call on all the Catholics in the group and arranged their transport to and from the nearest church, even providing them himself with breakfast after the service.

Later that winter all of us in the Dawkins' household fell victims to the 'flu. Irene Dawkins was expecting her third child and was not at all well. One night, when I was still pretty sick, Charles Dawkins rushed into my bedroom, asking me to go to his wife at once as she was in labour. He was off six miles to fetch the doctor because the 'phone was out of order. I tottered into Irene's room and found her obviously in pain, but looking far less green than I did, and she kindly asked me if I would like a drink of water, which I accepted!

In no time at all, and with nothing but moral support on my part, the baby was born. Mrs. Salmon, the excellent owner of the Ring of Bells, arrived at almost the same moment. She had seven children of her own so my troubles were over. The baby boy, David, was very small and premature, but I am glad to say that he thrived, and now, I hope, has children of his own.

One alarming incident will always remain in my memory. Although at that time Bristol had not been heavily bombed, there were spasmodic German raids throughout that winter. Compton Martin must have been in their flight path, and one night there was a mammoth explosion as a bomb fell just outside the village. What was so much worse was that, a moment or so later, the quiet night was pierced by one heartrending scream. A cottage on the outskirts had taken the full impact of the bomb, only one woman had survived, and it was she whom we heard with her appalling cry for help.

The following day was Sunday and while the children and I were in the village church it was shaken by another bomb explosion which sounded as if it were just beside it. At once I felt all the children's eyes on me, silently asking 'shall we go or stay'. I made reassuring motions and all went quiet once more. For the first time I realised how much the young rely on an adult's behaviour in times of crisis to trigger off their own reactions.

Fortunately, Compton Martin heard no more bombs while we were there. It was assumed that a German plane had discharged a couple on its return journey that first dreadful night, and destroyed one poor family in the process.

As I got to know the Fairbridge children better, I became concerned about one little boy of seven who seemed unsuited for life in the hurly-burly of a large farm school. Philip was a frail, timid child and under-sized for his age. By great good fortune he had been billeted with an elderly, childless couple in the village, where he found a warm, affectionate home. It was not long before these people consulted me about their strong desire to keep the little boy with them permanently. I supported this offer, and soon involved the Fairbridge Head Office in a long correspondence on the matter. Eventually it was agreed to withdraw Philip from emigration and to allow him to remain with his fosterparents. Many years later Philip brought his wife and two children to see me in Cornwall. Their well-being proved that in this case our decision had probably been the right one.

Early in the spring of 1940 there were indications from Gordon Green that the necessary permits for the children to sail to Canada would soon be forthcoming. I suppose my mind was full of these implications; one night I had a very vivid dream that a particularly nice Tyneside lad of eleven, another Joe, would not be going with us. So disturbing was the dream that next day I telephoned the Fairbridge office to ask for reassurance about Joe. I was told that although he seemed fit and in every way suitable for emigration, a medical report had just been received showing him to have a heart defect, which meant rejection by the Immigration authorities. Alternative plans had to be made for Joe in England, and before long we had to say goodbye.

35

At last the time came for the rest of us to leave Compton Martin for Canada. We were to sail from Liverpool on one of the Empress liners. Malcolm Jackson, an Australian who had worked for Fairbridge for some years was to be in charge of the party, while a girl called Deirdre Williamson and I were to help him.

The children and I had spent a happy cheerful ten months in Compton Martin, but they were all too excited about the adventure before them to worry about leaving, though I am sure that later on they remembered the kindness and affection they had received in the village.

It was an enormous help that by this time I knew our boys and girls so well. Again, Tynesiders predominated though there were some lively Londoners as well. Most were in the age range of eleven to fourteen, with a few much younger brothers and sisters. The eldest boy, nicknamed Lanky as he was so tall, was born in a Somerset workhouse and had grown up in a Children's Home there. Calmly he told me he was there because his mother was a Miss. Lanky's large size, good nature and attractive West Country burr made him one of the most popular boys in the group. Among the Cockneys were Harry Sharpe, who more than lived up to his name, Albert Bettoni who later became a champion boxer in Canada, while Gordon Neal personified the quick wit and sense of fun of the born East Ender. My secret favourite was Frankie Collins, a tough little eleven-year old from Tyneside, one of a large impoverished family. He was sent to seek his fortune overseas and I can only hope he found it.

Malcolm Jackson proved a cheerful, competent leader, and the sea crossing from Liverpool to Canada was a lot of fun and fortunately uneventful. The following week a passenger ship on the same route was lost through enemy action. Eighty-seven children were drowned and the British Government then stopped all overseas group sailings of children until the end of the war.

Once in Canada the ship sailed up the St. Lawrence river, and we went ashore at Quebec and Montreal to sample the delights of the cities. We gazed around Montreal from the highest building, sucking ice creams and looking at its ultra modern buildings, marvelling later at the wonders of the magic-eye doors, which I had never seen before. At the end of an exciting day we boarded the train which would take us through the Rockies to Vancouver city. The Canadian Pacific Railway provided us with a large coach which included our sleeping quarters and a dining area. Best of all, two splendid chefs, Fred and Joe, were already installed with the sole duty of cooking us excellent meals.

The journey took three days, with a twenty minute stop every four hours during the daytime. The train would draw into a small station and as soon as it stopped all the children would tumble out to race about the platform until the guard blew his whistle to warn us to return to our carriages. A feverish count by the escorts would then begin, and we always seemed to stick at twenty nine just as the train began to move. Miraculously number thirty would turn up just in time, and we could all breathe again until the next stop.

The sun shone for the whole trip. Below the track the waters of the Fraser river curved and sparkled, while the towering heights of the snow-covered Rockies loomed above us. We sometimes saw log cabins nestling on the mountain side, and once a real cowboy galloped in the distance. It was another world to us all.

We would start each day by one of the children reading a short psalm, this was followed by the Lord's Prayer. On our final morning in the train, Frankie Collins was the reader, he chose 'The Lord is my Shepherd, I shall not want....' I was moved almost to tears.

We were not able to see much of Vancouver city, as soon after our arrival we caught the ferry that was to take us to Vancouver Island. We reached Victoria quite late that day and found a coach waiting to take us on to the Prince of

Wales Fairbridge Farm School about two hundred miles inland.

The setting was superb, with the Cowichen River running through the farm land. The weather was still brilliantly fine and I slept out on the stoep of the little guest house, where big lilac trees were in full bloom, and visited by humming birds. Our new arrivals were given a very warm welcome and were soon made to feel at home in the cottages, which, as in Australia, were all under the care of a housemother. It was holiday time and we soon made our way to the river which was a great attraction. It reminded me of the Dart, with the same deep pools and smooth, round rocks, though in May the water was still icy.

My plans to travel home via the United States had been scrapped. News of the war became increasingly ominous, and though I was tempted to stay and work at the farm school, I decided to return to Britain without delay, while it still remained possible to do so.

I was terribly sorry to say goodbye to the boys and girls whom I had grown to know and like so well. They, too, were sad to lose their last link with home, but I had the comfort of knowing that they were in good hands with great opportunities before them.

As usual I travelled back steerage on one of the liners, most of the other passengers with me were seamen from Newfoundland who were going to join the Merchant Navy in Britain. One of them had a radio on deck and we all followed the war news anxiously. While we were still in mid-ocean we heard the BBC's announcement of the British Army's evacuation from the beaches at Dunkirk. I shall never forget the total silence on deck as this news came through. the men stood motionless around the radio, I think we all wondered whether the Germans would land in Britain before us.

Apart from this alarming news the sea trip was uneventful. After we had landed and had gone our separate ways,

Winston Churchill's famous broadcast gave us fresh hope and courage. It was certainly his finest hour.

Before leaving the subject of Child Migration I must refer to the newspaper articles which wrote of it with great hostility in the Sunday *Observer* in 1987, and in *The Guardian* in 1989. I felt impelled to write an article in defence which I sent to both papers. Neither of which decided to print it, nor in fact was it included in the social workers' paper, *Social Work Today*.

I cannot blame *The Observer*, as I do not take a Sunday paper, and it was some weeks' later that I was shown the articles, 'Lost Children of the Empire'. By the time I had written and posted my article, *The Observer* had naturally passed on to other subjects. I do in fact blame that excellent paper, *The Guardian*, as I sent it a copy of my article at once, after reading their's entitled, 'The Forgotten Children They Fed to the Empire'. Without being pompous I must protest that a good newspaper should be willing to print opposite views to their own, however unpopular these may be at a later date.

It is never wise to judge the work and ideals of one era on the standards of another, half a century later, if only because these may themselves be found to be equally flawed before another fifty or so years have passed.

Chapter 8
A trip to South Africa

There was nothing further I could do for The Fairbridge Society while the war lasted, but as I was pondering what to do next, I had a telephone call from Mrs. H.B. from London to say that her husband was to move from his post in the Middle East to Tokyo, where he had been appointed as First Secretary to the British Embassy. She and Diana were about to sail for Capetown, where they would stay until Mr. H.B. gave them the signal to join him in Japan.

Mrs. H.B. had rung to ask me to come out to South Africa in September to undertake Diana's education and to act as her friend and companion. My protestations that I would be quite unable to give this bright fifteen year old girl a decent education were brushed aside. Mrs. H.B. pleaded with me to take on the job for just on year. After that my return fare to the U.K. via any route of my choice would be paid, and rather weakly I accepted the bait. Only my passion for travel could explain this desertion of the war effort. Added to this, Britain had again lapsed into relative calm, and there were no indications that by September 18th, 1940, when I was due to sail for Capetown, the real war would have burst upon the country in the shape of the Blitz.

Mrs. H.B. had asked me to do a number of things for her in London, before I caught the night train to Glasgow to join the *Windsor Castle* bound for Capetown. London had been heavily bombed the night before my arrival, on the 17th, but I found an indefatigable taxi-driver and set off on my missions while buildings were still burning, and frequent detours were needed to avoid huge craters in the roads.

I had arranged to meet my sister, Marjorie, at King's Cross station before my train left for Glasgow, and I got there just in time, with all my chores completed, thanks to the pluck and ingenuity of my excellent taxi-driver.

40

It was good to have even a brief meeting with Marjorie before I left. She remained in Bethnal Green for the whole of the war, mercifully unscathed, but at this meeting I think we both wondered secretly whether we should ever meet again.

Marjorie had always been far less tough than the rest of my family and was always highly nervous. In spite of this she faced the hazards of the war and its effect in East London without a tremor. This, in spite of her job as a Voluntary Shelter Warden, which entailed going around the local air raid shelters at night, which I, for one, should have found most alarming. When I asked Marjorie how she could stand the awful proximity of the bombs, she replied that she never found them quite as frightening as the thought of meeting a bull in one of our Gower lanes.

Inevitably when it grew dark we heard the ominous wail of an air raid warning, all lights were extinguished as the crowded train slowly moved out of the station. To make matters worse, two very drunk Scandinavian seamen lurched into my already crowded carriage and squeezed their way in beside me. Not content with drinking freely from their whisky bottle, I was continually pestered to have a swig as well. After a pretty tiring day, this was nearly the last straw. Fortunately the other passengers in the carriage thought the same and before long a couple of them gently eased our exuberant friends into the corridor.

The journey to Glasgow was by no means a straightforward one and it seemed a lifetime before I finally got aboard the ship.

We left port in wild weather and for the first few days the seas were tremendously rough. I was not seasick but it was difficult to sleep at night while the cabin groaned and creaked.

The weather soon calmed down and by Sunday everyone tottered on deck for a short service. Our splendid Captain, later to be known as Eternity Brown, told us that we should be thankful for the very rough weather which had probably saved us from the attention of four submarines which were known to have been in the area.

I very much enjoyed the trip to Capetown. We were not allowed to land on Ascension Island, though it loomed like a large mushroom in still waters nearby.

The ship called at St. Helena where we all spent a day ashore. I walked through the sombre valley leading from the dock and thought of Napoleon and how he must have loathed the place. Returning to the ship I encountered the enormous tortoise, said to be over two hundred years old and treasured by the inhabitants for this reason. The creature looked very mournful as, indeed, its species tend to, though it was munching a large banana which reminded me of Winston Churchill's perpetual cigar, as it stuck out of his vast mouth before slowly disappearing completely.

Before we sailed, some of us got into trouble with the Captain for swimming from the ship while it was still at anchor. He told us that we might easily have lost an arm or a leg as menacing barracuda fish frequented the bay. However, we emerged unscathed and much refreshed as the weather was hot and oppressive.

I was lucky enough to get to know some interesting and amusing fellow passengers, in particular I enjoyed the company of three young women who were travelling out to join their husbands, who were in the Colonial Service and stationed in different parts of Africa. We often played lighthearted bridge, to pass the time, though what I most enjoyed was hearing of their lives in remote parts of Kenya and what was then Tanganyika. Joan D, whose husband was a District Officer was an excellent story teller. She had once been with him on safari among a tribe who mistook her for the Virgin Mary, as this was the only white woman of whom they had heard.

I was left with an urge to see Kilimanjaro and to climb the Mountains of the Moon.

The nearest I was to come to that was the spectacular view of Table Mountain with the Lion's Head and Devil's Peak ranged alongside in the serene waters of the bay, with Capetown spread along its base.

I had a very warm welcome from Diana and her mother when I landed. They were staying in the most attractive thatched hotel at St. James, one of the small coastal resorts which stretched along the coast from Capetown to the Naval base at Simonstown. I soon found that I had exchanged the real war in Britain for a lotus eating life of pleasure. Muezenberg beach provided swimming and surfing within a few minutes reach, while the heights of Table Mountain were a definite challenge.

Inevitably there were snags. I was warned not to go out alone. I, who had walked freely for miles in Europe, was for the first time confronted by the real or imagined dangers implicit in the colour bar. The nearby foothills of Table Mountain, covered with multi-coloured flowers in that glorious South African spring, seemed to beckon invitingly. I would sneak off to explore them when I could, in spite of dire warnings that I should meet with a fate worse than death.

I found the whole landscape exceedingly beautiful, though the flowers had little scent, nor did the fabulous multicoloured birds sing as sweetly as ours did in the garden at home. It soon became clear that our move to Tokyo would be further delayed, no doubt through a war-time hitch over Mr. H.B.'s posting to Japan. Mrs. H.B. rented a house in Rondebosch, nearer Capetown, and very wisely allowed Diana to attend an excellent day school there.

This left me entirely idle during term-time and I was able to take a hard look at the South African set up. Apart from the scenery, I did not like what I saw. The Cape coloured race which predominated in Capetown seemed to be treated with a fairly kindly contempt. I could discover no state system for the coloured children's education. I was told that schools would be wasted on such a degenerate

43

race, though from what I could see the boys and girls seemed lively and attractive.

I sensed a pervading fear between the white and coloured races, I could not help feeling that within the century a revolution of some kind was almost inevitable. I resolved that if I were ever to return to that country it would be as a Social Worker to try to help the coloured people, whom I thought to be bitterly and unfairly oppressed.

Mrs. H.B. was, as always, exceptionally kind and I made a number of good friends through her. Diana, too, now sixteen, was great fun to be with. She was an excellent mimic, and was soon able to take off the various accents around us, certainly the least lovely I have heard this side of Birmingham.

Its beautiful setting and wide streets, usually banked with stalls of flowers, made Capetown most attractive. It was, of course, a much smaller place then, and had not started to sprout buildings instead of flowers along the hillsides, as it was to do later.

The suburban railway train from Simonstown to Cape-town was usually crowded with British sailors on a spree. Some, who were a bit the worse for wear often through too much wine or beer, had to be helped back to the train by the Navy's huge Great Dane, Nuisance, who was provided with a first class ticket on the train for this purpose. Many a drunken sailor must have been saved a reprimand for late return by clinging to this friendly dog's collar and so guided back to the train, where comradely hands would heave him into a carriage.

The weather was glorious and I was anxious to climb to the top of Table Mountain before we left South Africa. There was no question of Diana coming with me. She was not athletic and though a good swimmer, mountaineering was not in her line. Through Mrs. H.B. I was linked up with two experienced Afrikaner mountaineers whom I met for the first time on the day we were to make our climb. I was

44

a little taken aback to see that both men were equipped with ropes and looked ready to tackle Mt. Everest. They, for their part, looked askance at my jersey, shorts and sandals, as I explained that my climbing experience was limited to scaling the rocks and cliff of my native Gower.

One of the men asked me whether I was nervous, and, like a fool, I said no. After a short discussion between the two of them, it was decided to take me on a category 'C' climb, which meant it would be of medium difficulty. All went well on the first easy stages, though I was gently reprimanded for using my hands and knees to climb, like a boy.

They were a friendly pair, the elder, a grizzled Afrikaner, was evidently a very skilled mountaineer. I thought it was most kind of them to spend a day with a beginner, when they would probably have chosen a more ambitious climb on their own.

It was not long before I was confronted by my worst test of nerves. We had arrived at the entrance to a small cave leading to a 200 foot chimney in a wall of rock inside the mountain. I was roped between the two men which gave me a faint sense of security, though the sight of the huge bunch of arum lilies growing away below us, seemed to strike a funereal note.

The leader showed me where to put my hands and feet on the sheer, wet, slippery rock, and though I was scared stiff I tried not to show it. We were now so high up that I dared not look down, when, to my horror, I saw my companion ahead of me adroitly cross over from one side of the chimney to the other.

There was nothing for it but to follow him over. I made an attempt to cross the narrow space, only to find that I could not reach the tiny hand-hold on the far side, so was left stranded on a thin ledge with what seemed like a bottomless abyss below me.

Even in this perilous dilemma I could not help being amused when the leader, seeing my predicament asked me if I was quite comfortable. I replied that this was the last way to describe my condition. Expertly he lowered his foot to make it possible for me to grasp it as I crossed the chasm. In a moment I was on the other side, though to this day I cannot think how I did it.

Nothing could have exceeded my sense of triumph and elation when we reached the summit, though I was terrified in case it was decided to make the descent the same way. Fortunately, after fully admiring the marvellous view which lay below us, we took a very easy route down.

As I thanked them both warmly when we said goodbye, they promised next time to take me up a far more difficult climb on the north face of the mountain, but for me, once was enough. I did have other climbs, though none that were so alarming. One night I got to the top of the Devil's Peak with a group of young people, to see Capetown and the whole coast brilliantly lit up below us.

Most of my swimming was in the warm sea at Muezenberg, but occasionally I went with friends to Sea Point, where the South Atlantic sweeps in to meet the Indian Ocean. There the water seemed icy though the hot, smooth rocks made a marvellous contrast. Bathing from them was tricky as one had to dodge the huge rollers before they crashed down on the rocks. Once I narrowly avoided disaster when a huge wave nearly took me with it. After that I kept to the warmer, safer beach at Muezenberg.

One day in Capetown I watched the arrival of several large convoys of soldiers who made a brief stay there en route, no doubt for one of the war zones. First marched in a batch of enormous Australians, followed by a regiment of even larger New Zealanders, while the British, of all shapes and sizes brought up the rear. Somehow what they lacked in size and splendour was made up for by their cheerful, perky gusto. Crowds lines the streets and cheered them all the way.

Early in 1941 I had time off to travel to the Transvaal to visit my uncle and aunt who had lived outside Ventersdorp near Johannesberg, for many years. Both were exceedingly patriotic (as only ex-patriots seem to be) and were suffering from the fact that all around them war-time sympathies were very much with Germany.

When the Union Jack raised by my aunt in her garden was pulled down, she spread it out on the law. I was devoted to them both, and it was a great reunion. My aunt was as Welsh as my own family, though she told me that she could only remember a few Welsh swear words then. My uncle was a county cricketer, and kept a very straight bat. They were delighted to see me looking plump and fit and showed me off in the neighbourhood as a proof that Britain was not starving.

We were soon joined by their son, Ivor, on leave from the R.A.M.C., who had spent a lot of time with us in Gower as a young man, and we all went by car to Durban, which he loved, as he was also a keen swimmer. It was good to see more of the continent. I was interested in the fine physique and independent bearing of the Zulus, and even remembered to buy a postcard at Ladysmith to send to a splendid old Zulu who, after a lifetime as a steel worker in Llanelli, had retired to live near us on the Pennard Cliffs. He had told me that he was born in Ladysmith and had worked as a lion tamer at Sanger's Circus before landing up in Llanelli. I heard later that he treasured my postcard until he died.

After this splendid holiday I returned to Rondebosch, only to hear soon that my home town, Swansea, had been devastated by three nights of terrible air raids early in 1941. I decided that it was high time for me to return to Britain to try to find something to do to help the war effort instead of surfing and sitting to the sun.

There still seemed no prospect of Mrs. H.B. and Diana moving to Tokyo, and though she was very angry at my desertion, I simply could not put up with such an idle life any longer. I did feel guilty about letting them down, and I am afraid Mrs. H.B. never forgave me; in spite of this my mind was made up and I telephoned the Capetown shipping agent to ask to be booked on the next ship to leave for Britain.

I was told that a berth had been provisionally booked for me on a ship that was likely to arrive at Capetown within the next six weeks or so. I was now most anxious to be gone, and pressed the agent to let me know at once if, through cancellation, I could get an earlier ship.

It was not long before I had a phone call from the Shipping Office to say there had been a cancellation of a berth on the SS *Ulysses* which I could have providing I could get on board within the next three hours. I made a quick calculation and accepted this offer, though after six months in South Africa it meant a tremendous rush to be on board in time.

As soon as I heard the ship's name I knew it was the one for me. My brother, Vernon, was a poet, and had instilled in me a lifelong love of poetry. Some of my favourite poems were in French, among them, and high on the list was one of DuBellay's with its famous first line:-

'*Heureux qui comme Ulysse a fait un beau voyage*'

I could only feel that it was a good omen. After hastily packing and kissing Diana goodbye, I hurried aboard.

Chapter 9
Ulysses returns

The ship was crammed with Australian and New Zealand men, the former mostly already airmen who were going to join the RAF. Although there were only about a dozen women on board, I had to share a four berth cabin with three others. One, an enormously fat Afrikaner, had been given a top berth while I had a lower one. I immediately offered to change with her and was rewarded by her overwhelming thanks. We soon became friends and I learned that she and her husband, who were Dutch Reform Church missionaries ran a leper colony in West Africa. They had just taken their seven year old only son to start school in South Africa.

Although they only travelled as far as Freetown with me, and I cannot even remember their names, this woman remains in my memory as a shining example of devoted service and humanity. Always cheerful and uncomplaining she bore no resentment against the British though her father had been killed in the Boer War. Her husband, however, obviously disliked the British and never spoke to me at all.

I was sorry to say goodbye to my fat friend when we reached Freetown about a week later, where a number of other civilian passengers also left the ship. I had expected the Ulysses to sail on without delay, but it was another week before a convoy formed and we started off again.

During our wait in Freetown I heard that the ship on which I had originally been booked to sail had passed us and sailed on alone. For the first time I regretted my change of plan, but when I heard, through the grapevine, a few days later, that this ship had been sunk, I thanked my good angel that I was safe in the *Ulysses.*

Once or twice, to relieve the tedium of waiting, some of us went ashore in a ship's tender to visit Freetown. It was hot and dusty and I cannot recall seeing much of interest, though on one occasion we did have an amusing experience returning to the ship. Half way across, in a clear, calm sea, we saw a motor boat steering straight towards us. It appeared deserted, but when, in spite of our helmsman's efforts, there was a slight collision, half-a-dozen stark naked Africans popped up on deck from below, gesticulating wildly. We assumed the poor fellows were asleep, drunk or sober. No harm was done, though the incident taking place as it did, in a perfectly calm, empty sea, was a real diversion and made us all laugh.

At last the convoy of about a dozen ships was assembled, the Admiral boarded the Ulysses as she was to be the Commodore's ship, and we were off moving, I would estimate, at about 7 knots. In fact I thought I might well have kept up with it swimming at a steady breast stroke.

I now found myself sitting at the doctor's table for meals, in the company of four Australian pilot officers. Their backgrounds and personalities could not have been more different. I liked them all, but my favourite was a quiet young man who had worked in a garage in Western Australia before he earned his pilot's commission from the ranks. I felt that if I were to fall overboard, Hugo, as he was called, would be the first to pull me out. I knew that all my companions were destined to fly bombers in Britain, and though I never saw any of them again once we had left the ship, when the first daylight raid on Berlin was filmed and shown on the *Movietone News*, there was Hugo among the crew. I heard that he became famous as an air ace in Australia but finally went missing as so many brave young men did in those days.

We had strict instructions to carry our life jackets at all times. They seemed to be made of stiff cork and I soon grew to dislike mine very much. The Australians who loved to tease me, said that in case of the worst, the jacket would break one's neck on impact with the water. Naturally I lost all confidence in the thing, and was told off three times by the Admiral for not carrying it with me.

Safety drill on board was a daily priority. We all had to report at our allocated stations on a given signal. I found that mine was on the top deck, which did not seem at all handy if we had to abandon the ship. My Australian friends comforted me by saying that there would be absolute chaos in any case and that the greatest danger was from sharks. They were all fine swimmers and I noticed they carried knives in their belts in case of the worst.

In spite of the obvious dangers no one seemed to be in the least afraid, I have always loved the sea, which never seemed to me to be as much of threat as being buried by bombs or falling buildings on land.

The weeks passed and on we sailed, weaving about, no doubt, to avoid any lurking submarines. One dark, starlit night I suddenly became aware that the ship's engines had stopped. Like everyone else, I hurried on deck just in time to see the dark shape of a destroyer loom up alongside. In no time a gangway was run along between the two ships, allowing a number of shipwrecked survivors to come aboard the *Ulysses*. Everything was done in total silence, which made the scene even more dramatic. As soon as the last man had left the gangway, the destroyer moved off as quietly as she had come, followed only by our waves and good wishes. Some of the survivors had been in open lifeboats for up to six weeks, and though the *Ulysses* was now full to bursting, they were warmly welcomed and thankful to be in comfort and comparative safety.

The weather was still warm and calm, though we had no idea where we were. The Australians passed the time in gambling; I talked and paced the decks and played deck games. Most of the men had spent two months at sea, and boredom was a problem.

One day a tug-of-war was arranged between the Australians and the New Zealanders. There were enormous men in both teams, but the New Zealanders won, largely through the huge man at base, who simply sat on the end of the rope and could not be shifted.

As we moved into the most dangerous waters we were instructed that on the blast of one whistle we were to go to our cabins, collect any valuables that would fit into a small case and wait there. A second whistle would be to abandon ship, when we should all go to our allotted stations. Even this grim development had its uproarious side, if only to see the extraordinary things the passengers were prepared to take with them. One man, I remember, festooned himself with every imaginable kitchen utensil so that he looked like a replica of Alice's White Knight. One day there were eight alarm whistles, but luckily for us the second fatal blast was never blown.

Just as it seemed that we must be nearing Britain, and the Australians chief concern was that after nearly three months at sea they had drunk the ship dry, an aeroplane flew in low from nowhere, dropped three bombs on the convoy and disappeared again into the blue. At first it looked as through no ship had been hit until slowly the last cargo boat in the convoy began to tilt over and finally sank. Fortunately the crew were all rescued, and though we waited for the plane's return to do more damage, it never came.

After three months at sea, including eight weeks from Capetown, the brave *Ulysses* brought us safely into dock at Liverpool. I said fond farewells and good wishes all round (and how they needed them) to my shipboard companions, and hurried off to catch the first train home to Wales. My joy and relief at finding my parents and brother safe and sound were only exceeded by theirs, as their last news of me had been in March, and now it was June 1941, when shipping losses at sea through enemy action were probably at their worst.

It was sad to see the centre of Swansea in ruins, but Gower at least remained intact. An unexploded bomb had been reported one night to my parents as it was very near their house. Their typical reaction had been to open all windows and to return to bed.

I have no doubt that they slept the sleep of the just.

Chapter 10
Social work in Plymouth

Determined to do my duty, I called at the Swansea Labour Exchange without delay. I was told that a Social Worker was urgently needed by the Plymouth Guild of Social Service, where three nights of continuous bombing had devastated the city centre. Help was needed to administer the Air Raid Relief Fund just set up by the Mayor, Lord Astor, and to open a Citizens' Advice Bureau with the immediate aim of tracing missing relatives after the raids. I travelled to Plymouth at once and was met by the Guild's President, the late Mr. J.J. Judge, an old man then and reminiscent in every way of J.M. Barrie's eccentric Mr. Lobb in the play, *Dear Brutus*. I took to him immediately.

As we walked to the Barbican Mr. Judge told me that the Guild was a voluntary charity run by a local council with a very small staff headed by Miss Glover, a splendid old lady who was to teach me a lot. Her two assistants were also elderly; after my appointment (there were no other applicants) I began to feel rather like a character in 'Cranford'. The atmosphere in the Guild's offices was staid, Victorian and unworldly.

There was no question of lodgings or hotel accommodation at that time, but Mr. Judge invited me to stay at the Virginia House Settlement in the Barbican, where a number of social workers and youth leaders were already taking refuge after being bombed out of their previous homes. I immediately felt at ease in the settlement, which was run by Stephen and Mary Dalston, both delightful Quakers, with plenty of humour and a quiet competence unshaken by the air raids and consequent upheaval of the City three days earlier. I had arrived feeling ready for anything but with what I could only feel was my usual luck, Plymouth was never blitzed again, though slight air raids were experienced from time to time.

Among the friends I made at Virginia House was Elizabeth Yeo, then a Youth Club Leader employed to run clubs for young people still living in the City. Although my work for the Guild kept me busy all day, it was not long before Elizabeth talked me into running a Club for young boys in Plymouth, whose main delight was in boxing, and who called themselves Hell's Angels.

I had never liked that sport, but I very much enjoyed the company of these eleven to fourteen year old boys and the link with Elizabeth started a friendship which was to last all our lives.

My days were spent in organising the C.A.B. which had been set up in a Nissen hut in the centre of the City. Ruins surrounded it, but the people of Plymouth seemed quite undaunted, and on fine summer evenings there was even dancing on the Hoe.

One of my jobs was to sort out endless appeals for help from the Lord Mayor's Fund from people who had suffered loss or damage in the air raids. This entailed quite a lot of visiting, which I enjoyed.

One of the most curious applications I had was from an old man who had played the drums in the Playhouse Theatre orchestra, and when his drums were lost in the bombing, he felt, like Othello, that his occupation was gone. I gave him all the help I could over claiming war damage, and was successful in getting a small grant from the Lord Mayor's Fund. We became good friends, and I kept in touch with him and his wife long after I had left Plymouth.

In the height of summer I decided to look for somewhere outside the City to live. I really liked Plymouth, but much preferred country life to any other. Cycling round the coast at the weekend I came to Wembury, and was greatly attracted by the old Mill House on the shore. It was then being run as a cafe by a girl called Barbara, whose husband was in the Navy, overseas. Over a cup of coffee I asked Barbara if she had a room to let, and was delighted when she told me that she was on her own and would welcome another woman living in the house.

I moved in shortly afterwards, unperturbed by the fact that I would have to cycle eight of the hilliest miles in Britain to get to my office every day. There were buses from Wembury, but as I always preferred action to waiting, I usually cycled to and from the town.

I loved Wembury. Apart from the small church on the cliffs ours was the only building on the shore, and although the beach was closed by barbed wire entanglements, Barbara and I would eel our way through them for a bathe whenever the sea was reasonably calm.

On fine evenings when I was free, we would often walk along the deserted cliffs, accompanied by Barbara's airedale bitch, and, for a short distance, her seven cats would also stroll along.

Every week the Mill House was invaded by a group of Marine Biologists from Plymouth, who were doing highly secret work on the shore. I used to accuse them of playing, and said that they should be ashamed of fishing around in rock pools, as I was so used to doing for fun in Gower. They were delightful people and took my teasing in very good part. I knew, of course, that their work was of infinite value, and was sorry when I left the area not to see them again.

In the meantime my work at the Guild of Social Services was running into rough water. Looking back I can see that my energy and immaturity were really to blame. Although I had infinite sympathy and understanding for the unfortunate applicants who came to the Guild and the C.A.B. for help, this dwindled perceptibly when I worked with some of the good ladies who formed the bulk of our voluntary helpers. No doubt they found me bossy and tiresome, if not a dangerous revolutionary, while I dismissed a lot of them as middle class blimps.

There is an old Welsh saying about certain pit ponies which would lonly lead from the front, for my part I have always found it difficult to work well under too much control and constraint and as I was so much younger than everyone else on the staff, this was an added difficulty.

After twelve months my dear old friend Mr. Judge had the unpleasant task of calling me to order. Without more ado I gave in my notice, and though we remained the best of friends for years, I always said afterwards that, for the only time in my life, if I had not been a fast talker I might have been sacked.

I still retain my affection for Plymouth and warm admiration for its cheerful, stalwart people. When I catch a glimpse of the Mew Stone on my visits to that area, I remember how I used to hurtle down the steep hill to Wembury on my bicycle and was always so glad to see its beautiful triangular shape in the distance at sea, and to know that I was nearly home.

Chapter 11
Wales in wartime

It was sad to say goodbye to Barbara to say nothing of her dog and innumerable cats, but once away I flew like a homing pigeon to my beloved Gower, where my parents gave me their usual warm welcome.

My brother, Vernon, had joined the RAF but our London evacuee, Denis Balkin, was still with us, and by this time quite established as one of the family. Marjorie had been appointed as one of the ten Ministry of Health's Regional Welfare Officers for the homeless and was still living in Bethnal Green where she also worked as a voluntary Shelter Welfare Officer at night.

I returned to the Swansea Labour Exchange for further instructions. This time I was directed to a bomb factory, where the firm was, for the first time, employing women as well as men and wanted a Welfare Officer to look after its women employees. The factory was in Landore, then a grey, desolate area outside Swansea, so grim that when our friends arrived in Swansea by train we always advised them to close their eyes for the last twenty minutes of the journey. I arrived at the factory by bus and was shown round the premises by a very nice young manager. I tried not to show how awful I thought the place. I was reminded at once of pictures of Dante's Inferno, the heat and noise were bad enough, but the sight of masked men armed with what looked like long pitchforks moving round the vast dark premises really was reminiscent of an imagined hell.

Even so, I was willing to accept the job until the Manager told me that he wanted someone to work there on a permanent basis, and some guarantee that I would continue in employment after the end of the war. I had to confess that wild horses would not retain me there a minute after hostilities ended, and we parted by mutual agreement, to my great relief.

I was much luckier on my next call at the Labour Exchange, where I was advised to apply to the Welsh Board of Health in Cardiff for a post as a Billeting Inspector. There had been a considerable fuss in the Press and in Government circles over a series of frauds in the Evacuation Service through people with whom evacuees had been placed, drawing money for their keep long after the evacuees had left them.

As a result of this scandal, the Ministry of Health had decided to appoint Billeting Inspectors to be responsible for making wide-spread checks in the Reception areas in order to detect and prevent fraud. Four Billeting Inspectors were to be appointed to cover the whole of Wales and I was sent off to the Head Office of the Welsh Board of Health in Cardiff to be interviewed for one of them.

I knew a little about the Evacuation Service through my experiences with the Fairbridge children in Compton Martin, but I failed to answer several of the questions put to me by the late Dr. D.J. Roberts, who interviewed me. However, applicants were scarce, and I was given the job. I did stipulate that as the duties of a Billeting Inspector could hardly be called welfare work, I should be considered for any suitable vacancy that might arise in social work later on.

Almost immediately four women, including myself, were appointed as Billeting Inspectors, two were to cover North Wales and two South. I was amused to find that my new colleagues knew even less than I did about the Evacuation Service. After only two weeks intensive training at the Head Office we were posted to various branch offices in Wales, and let loose on the unsuspecting Local Authorities in the Reception Areas.

I found to my delight that I was to work from the Swansea office and that my region would stretch from there to Aberystwyth. Like most girls of my age and upbringing I was totally ignorant of the work of Local Government. I was now expected to tackle a host of Billeting Officers and Treasurers in all the Rural and Urban Councils in my area.

The work entailed visiting these offices, checking their billeting records and then making random checks on households in which evacuees had been placed to make sure that they were, in fact, still there. The post office provided us with receipts of payments for evacuees in each area, which we could check against our visits. These sacred objects had to be returned later to the Head Office without fail.

Armed with a large brief case for the first time in my life, I set out to inspect the billeting records of a large Rural Council outside Swansea. Like most civilians in war time I had to use public transport whenever possible, this entailed walking to the various billets that I had to visit.

On this, my very first appearance as a Billeting Inspector, the weather was showery when I emerged from the Council Offices to do my visits, and as the rain came I stopped in a country lane to put on my mackintosh; while I was doing this, I put my brief case, which contained among other things the sacred Post Office receipts, on a hedge for a moment, and then walked on without it.

After about a quarter of a mile I felt that something was missing and galloped back the way I had come, in a state of acute anxiety. Fortunately I found the brief case intact, just where I had left it, but I never forgot this near escape from absolute disaster which made me very much more careful in future.

On another occasion I was caught in a very heavy rainstorm and when a car stopped to offer me a lift I accepted it willingly. It was not long before I realised by the erratic driving and an ominous clanking of bottles in the boot that both the driver and his male companion were drunk. Not only this, but they were not driving in the direction in which I wanted to go, and seemed if anything to increase their speed when I pointed this out. Fortunately, I soon saw that we were approaching a pub. Quick as light I suggested that we should all stop for a drink. The car came to a halt, I leapt out and told the driver what I thought of him. It was the last lift I ever accepted while I was working, in fact it left me with a marked distaste for hitch-hiking.

I found the work interesting. The hard pressed Local Government officials in the billeting world in West Wales were nearly all courteous and friendly. A number were also employed by their Local Authorities as Housing Officers and showed real insight and concern over the evacuees they dealt with. There were, of course, very different levels of competence between some of the large and small Authorities. No doubt it added an almost impossible burden to the smaller Urban Councils to be expected to keep exact billeting records when faced with so many other war time emergencies. Nor was there much love lost between Central and Local Government, and it said a lot for the patience of the officials I met that I was nearly always treated with great civility.

One exception was the irate Treasurer of one of my smallest Councils in West Wales. When I pointed out the chaotic billeting records in his department he glared at me through his spectacles, across his desk, and declared loudly that he would have me know that Kidwelly was a Chartered Borough Council before Whitehall was even thought of. I was tempted to reply that their methods did not seem to have changed much since then, but thought better of it and beat an ignominious retreat.

It was a great pleasure to me to get to know the beautiful area of West Wales, and to meet so many different people in it. I never found any fraud, but was often disturbed by gaps in the Evacuation Welfare Services, which I reported to the Head Office. My boss there, Mr. H. Burgess, a very intelligent Londoner with a quirkly sense of humour, would advise me to keep my eye on the billeting records and not be diverted by welfare causes, which were not my concern.

Early in 1943 I was advised of an impending vacancy for a Regional Welfare Officer in West Wales, to advise and help the Local Authorities in that area with any problems arising in the Evacuation Service. I applied for the job at once, as this was just the sort of work I wanted. Once again I was interviewed by Dr. Roberts and was given the appointment. I was to cover the same area but this time I was based at the Head Office in Cardiff, where I shared a large office with two other Welfare Officers and five other secretaries and typists. Although they were all very nice people, they smoked like chimneys and the clatter of the typewriters seemed continuous. Fortunately, I was usually only in the office on Mondays and Fridays and spent the rest of the week in the fresher air of West Wales.

Like most of the Welsh administrative offices in Cardiff, our huge Noah's Ark of a building was in Cathays Park right in the centre of the City. I was amused to find the War Office next door, housed in what had previously been the headquarters of the Temple of Peace. I never understood its previous functions before its wartime transformation.

My father had been born and brought up in an old house, Tynewydd at Gwaelod-y-Garth, about six miles from Cardiff, where my uncle, John Phillips and his delightful daughter, Nest, were still living. Through their infinite kindness, Tynewydd became a second home to me whenever I was in Cardiff and I shall never forget their endless hospitality, the splendid care of their friend and housekeeper, Morfy, who remained with them for over fifty years and the hilarious fun we all had.

My usual routine was to call on various Local Authorities in West Wales during the week and to return to Cardiff on Fridays to report and sort out any difficulties that I had come across. Needless to say, there were plenty of these, particularly over the housing of mothers and young children from the Cities.

I was fascinated to get a birds-eye view of the workings of a large Central Government Department, even though, as a temporary civil servant. I was allowed far more latitude than the permanent staff. I liked the atmosphere of the place, which was both friendly and democratic.

62

The heads of departments were an intelligent lot and easy to work with though I sometimes fell out with some of the medical staff, who seemed much less flexible in their ideas.

The greatest friend I made there was a Canadian Social Worker, Alice Carroll, who was one of a batch of twenty four Social Workers sent over from Canada to help with the British Evacuation Service. Alice was one of the two women sent to work in Wales. She was a warm, delightful person, basically very serious, her strong sense of humour was always breaking through. Alice's work was confined to helping maladjusted children, and as we covered the same area in West Wales, we often came into contact.

Whenever we could, we arranged to be in the same fire watching rota at weekends, when some staff were always on duty in the Welsh Board of Health's main office. Fire watching was not normally an onerous job, as we usually played table tennis in the basement until bedtime when the sexes would divide and retire to improvised bedrooms on the same floor, and where a porter was instructed to call us if there was an air raid. The Chairman, Mr. W. Armer, (later to be knighted) was a keen table tennis player and would often join us in the basement, his favourite opponent was one of the hall porters who also played a very good game. Unlike Whitehall, the Welsh Board of Health was pleasantly democratic, and the high and low mixed in well together, and we all shared the same canteen.

Cardiff was spared the fate of Swansea in the matter of air raids, though from time to time bombs would fall. On one such occasion when Alice and I were fire watching a bomb fell so near our building that all the lights were put out. I am ashamed to say that we were all caught unawares as we groped our way upstairs, though I did have the wit to ask the porter if there was no alternative method of lighting the building. He replied rather dubiously that 'there was only the emergency lighting now.' Stifling my amusement I said that this was an emergency and soon the lights were on.

Nothing more happened this time, but later in the year incendiaries fell on the building and our Chairman was among those who climbed onto the roof to help put out the fires.

Another democratic feature was that there was no high table in the canteen, and as most of the staff used it, I came into contact with a number of people I might not otherwise have met. The longer I worked there the more I admired the work of the civil service in Wales, as far as I experienced it in my small section. The only weakness that I could see in the system was that promotion of the permanent staff seemed to rely on a person's years of service rather than on merit, but this, I think, is no longer so.

Chapter 12
The Evacuation Service & Regional Welfare Work

In 1943 when I began work as a Regional Welfare Officer things were pretty quiet in the Evacuation Services. While large numbers of evacuees, both unaccompanied children and women with young families had long since returned to their homes, those that remained had settled down with varying degrees of contentment in the Reception Areas.

Once again my work involved visiting the Rural and Urban District Councils in West Wales though in a different capacity. My objects were to advise and help the Billeting Authorities over the various problems thrown up by their evacuees. I was also concerned with the quality of care being provided and took every occasion I could to visit individual homes and judge for myself the well being of the children and young families now so dependent on Welsh hospitality.

From time to time a file marked M.P. Priority would arrive on my desk in Cardiff. This meant that a Member of Parliament had raised a question in the House about a complaint he had received from his constituancy regarding the plight of one or more evacuees in Wales.

However trivial the complaint seemed there was no time to be lost in dealing with these vital documents. Investigation and a report had to be made immediately. I remember one occasion when parents in London had complained to their M.P. that their two children who were billeted in the wilds of Cardiganshire were being fed entirely on porridge.

I travelled nearly a hundred miles before arriving at their very homely billet where I met the healthy, friendly country-woman who was caring for them. I made no complaint but introduced myself as a Welfare Officer anxious to see how the London children were progressing. In due course I was able to ask how the rations were going. "Well", said their hostess, "before going to school they have a lovely bowl of porridge...." The mid-day meal was taken at school and I heard with inward amusement that when the children came home they had a lovely bowl of porridge. At this point the children arrived home looking remarkably fit and happy.

I wrote an accurate report of this encounter stating that while it was true that porridge loomed large on the menu, the children certainly seemed to be thriving on it. I added that the people of Cardiganshire had a very limited diet during the war and the children fared no worse than everyone else. Above all, they seemed well and happy.

It is easy to forget more than half a century later, the appalling conditions in which many evacuees first arrived in Wales from London, Birmingham and in particular, Liverpool. Apart from totally inadequate clothing, lice, scabies and impetigo on the new arrivals greatly shocked their country hosts. Bed-wetting seemed at one time an almost universal problem. Not surprisingly some householders simply failed to cope, though the majority turned to manfully, frequently spending their own money to buy their evacuees clothing. The weekly billeting allowance of 10/6d did not go far, parents in the cities were supposed to be responsible for their children's clothing needs, but many failed even to keep in touch with them by letter, never having had the need to use a pen much before.

Local Billeting Officers were beset with problems. The worst was bed-wetting. One cannot wonder that children, up-rooted from their homes and families, sometimes also untrained in every way, suffered from this complaint, but for households unused to it, it was hard to bear.

Rubber sheeting was doled out by the mile, but in the end the Government had to provide Evacuation Hostels to accommodate chronic bed wetters and other misfits.

Patterns of really serious misbehaviour among a relatively small number of evacuees caused disruption in the Reception Areas quite out of proportion to the size of the problem. There were regular meetings at the Welsh Board of Health in Cardiff between social workers, psychiatrists and psychologists to discuss the best way to tackle these children's needs. As a result the first hostels for maladjusted children were set up in Wales, the cost being met by Central Government.

Harassed Billeting Officers found it very difficult to persuade householders to accommodate mothers with young children. An easier solution was to requisition houses which could accommodate several families. The result was the isolation of the city dwellers from their new neighbours in the country and hostilities were often latent even if they did not always break out.

My business was to try to spread oil on troubled waters, but one of the saddest visits I had to make was to a remote country mansion in Pembrokeshire which was being used to house old and infirm men and women from Stepney. Although the staff did everything possible for these old people's comfort, their homesickness for East London was really pitiful to see. As soon as they learned on my visit that my sister worked in Bethnal Green and that I knew that part of London well, I was welcomed as a dear friend and ally.

I reassured them all that it would not be too long before the end of the war would allow them to return to their beloved City, even though I felt some doubts as to whether many of them would make it. I visited one poor old dear who had been sent to the hospital wing of a local workhouse. She clutched me by the arm, with desperate pleading that I should get her transferred to a London hospital. There was nothing I could do. I left convinced that the older the victim, the more cruelly the dogs of war could bite.

Like all my colleagues I was concerned that so many young mothers and children soon left the Reception Areas to return to the danger zone when things there seemed a bit quieter. I used to discuss this when I met my sister, Marjorie, who, as a Regional Officer for the Homeless in London was often on the receiving end of the problem. Marjorie told me that on one occasion when she asked a woman, who had just returned to London, why she had left the safety of the country, the reply she got was, "It was all that grass, Miss, it fair go me down".

A propos of nothing, during these latter years of the war, Marjorie and I met more than once at conferences in Whitehall, which concerned us both as Regional Welfare Officers - she for the London HOmeless, and myself as part of the Ministry's Evacuation Service. I need hardly say that (though I thought Whitehall a bit stuffy, after the democratic atmosphere of the Welsh Board of Health) we both enjoyed these unexpected meetings enormously.

Just as everything seemed quiet on the west Wales front, news came of the evacuation of the South Coast of England in preparation for the invasion of France.

Whereas the sudden arrival of thousands of evacuees had been accepted by their astonished hosts with surprise and resignation, in 1944 it was a different matter. Experienced Billeting Officers were able to cope with the new hordes of unaccompanied children without too much difficulty, but wrung their hands in despair when told to expect large number of mothers with young children.

I was in our Head Office one Friday when volunteers were called for that weekend to help the distraught Billeting Officer for Cardiff, where, instead of the five hundred unaccompanied children he had been told to expect, the same number of young families had arrived that day. These unfortunate people had been temporarily housed in the large Chapel vestries which abounded in the City, and volunteers were asked for to search Cardiff for more suitable private accommodation for them.

68

As one of these I was sent to Whitchurch, a highly respectable residential area in Cardiff with ample housing, I thought, to house the whole British Army. Behind a large chapel I found a miserable crowd of women and small children crowded into the vestry, where the little ones screamed their opinion of the situation in no uncertain terms.

When I pleaded on my house-to-house visits to householders to find room for a family in need of shelter I met with far more Pharisees than good Samaritans. Rather naturally people were sick and tired of the demands made on them by the war, and I returned to the vestry on Sunday morning to find it still crowded. Before long the bells sounded for the morning service and I was astonished to see the sedate congregation file into the chapel with not a glance at the sea of misery behind them in the vestry.

When a message was sent round there asking for the children to be kept quiet during the service, it was all I could do not to bound up to the pulpit and point out to the congregation where their Christian duty lay.

Next day I had to go off to West Wales, so I never heard the end of the story. No doubt the families were eventually found somewhere to live, but if ever there was a lost opportunity to do good, it was at that Whitchurch chapel.

As a complete contrast and what was certainly a happier occasion, I was sent as the Ministry's Observer to one of the railway stations in the Rhondda Valley, where a train-load of families from the south coast was due to arrive. I was touched to see that a string of flags had been erected overhead, while crowds of cheering folk gave the newcomers a warm welcome when the train pulled in.

I learned later that over 20,000 evacuees found homes in the Rhondda Valley, in spite of its poor, inadequate housing at that time. Perhaps it was the fact that the people living there had themselves suffered want and poverty that made them so willing to help others in need.

Yet again I was asked to report on the arrival of another train-load of mothers and young children from the south coast, this time in one of the most remote parts of west Wales.

The train was late and it was pitch dark when it finally trundled into the station which was far too small to accommodate half the coaches. After a thirteen-hour journey the exhausted women and children had to jump onto the lines, and trailed like the retreat from Moscow, in a dejected group to the improvised Reception Centre. Small wonder that so many preferred to confront any possible danger in their own home areas, rather than endure the loneliness they found in this remote part of Wales, where they could not even count on all the people around them speaking English.

Most child evacuees adapted quickly to their new surroundings, and city children in particular were usually quick to enjoy country life. Not so their poor mothers who sometimes found that the only familiar, friendly place in an village was the pub. It was not then customary in rural Wales for women to frequent such places, with the result that the newcomers got a bad mark for unseemly behaviour, instead of the help and friendship that they really needed.

Chapter 13
Billeting problems

I was free to plan my own work providing I left a weekly written programme indicating where I would be each day so that I could be contacted if a urgent problem arose. I was in Carmarthen when I had a telegram from the Chairman of the Welsh Board of Health asking me to telephone him immediately. To say that I read this command with dismay would be an understatement. It was unheard of for the. Chairman to contact any of his lowly subordinates direct, and inevitably I tried to think of what I must have done wrong.

However, when I rang Mr. Armer I was told that Carmarthen Borough was in a state of seige and had refused point blank to find billets for nearly a hundred boys recently evacuated from an Independent Grammar School in Dover. The Welsh Board of Health had responded to this act of open rebellion by offering to lend one of its staff to act as the Council's Billeting Officer until all the boys had been found homes, or if this offer was refused, to accept the alternative which would be for the Welsh Board of Health to take over full responsibility for the Evacuation Service in that area.

The Council members decided to accept the loan of a Billeting Officer as the lesser evil, and the Chairman of the Welsh Board of Health asked me if I would take on the job. I have never been able to resist a challenge and agreed to accept this one, though I did stipulate that I should return to Cardiff to discuss the project with him before embarking on this rather daunting task.

I learned from one of the Department's Solicitors in Cardiff that three of Carmarthen's most prominent citizens had already been taken to court after refusing to accept evacuees in their homes, but that the cases had failed on a technicality. My first task would be to take these three

71

unworthies back before the Magistrates and to see that they were properly dealt with.

I returned rather thoughtfully to Carmarthen, where I booked a comfortable room in the Bear Hotel. I felt I should need a good base for my mission, and the name seemed appropriate.

My first step was to ask the Clerk of the Borough Council to call a meeting of all the members, when this was arranged I appealed to them to set a good example to the town by each of them offering a home to an evacuee. Not one agreed to do so. I could not delay action in re-starting the billeting process in respect of the householders who had previously appeared in Court, as our Cardiff Solicitor was standing by for a re-run of the cases.

What disturbed me was that, in order to comply with the law, it was essential to serve a child as well as a billeting notice at the home of a householder, after which his refusal might end in prosecution. I did not at all relish subjecting any child to such an experience, but it had to be done, if an example was to be set in the town.

I made myself known to the Dover School's Headmaster, who was quick to see me as an ally, though unfortunately his lack of tact and rather pompous manner had not found favour with the people of Carmarthen. We made our way to one of the Chapel vestries where over sixty large, bored boys were waiting to be found homes.

The impending invasion of France by our forces was one of the best kept secrets of the war; no wonder that the townspeople in west Wales could not understand why they should be asked to give homes to a lot of husky lads from the south coast, all of whom seemed to have very adequate places to live in around Dover. No one suspected the mammoth preparation in hand by the War Office, or that the forces had descended in thousands on that very place, in preparation for the imminent invasion of France.

I decided that the best plan was to invite the boys' co-operation in order to find a volunteer to go with me when I served notices on the three recalcitrant householders. I explained the legal requirements and assured the boys that there was not the least likelihood of anyone being offered a home with any of them. I added bribery as another incentive, with an offer of half-a-crown to the boy finally chosen to help me. They all listened attentively, and to my delight, responded enthusiastically to the plan. I finally selected a large 14-year old boy nicknamed Lazy Smith from a number of volunteers.

We set off in due course to serve a billeting notice and a boy on our chosen victims. This was not as easy as it sounds as the law required that the billeting notice must be served (with boy) direct to the householder. It was a case of once bitten, twice shy, as the wary householders were most reluctant to open their front doors. Lazy Smith played his part with gusto and enjoyment, dashing from one door to another until we were successful in gaining access.

All three householders again refused to accept the boy and later the Solicitor from the Welsh Board of Health brought them before the Magistrates for a second time. They were found guilt, though this only resulted in derisory fines.

It was weeks before, with pleading and coercion, I was able to find all the Dover boys homes. I found it reassuring that after the initial reluctance and hostility towards the evacuees, the boys were quickly accepted into their new homes with apparent kindness and, in many cases, what grew into real affection.

An even harder task was to find a suitable person willing and able to take on the job of Billeting Officer to the Borough in my place. Eventually a woman came forward and was accepted by the Borough Council as my replacement. I was glad to leave Carmarthen after six weeks of really hard work. I do not doubt that my pleasure was fully shared by the Council members.

73

Ironically, my mother had grown up in Carmarthen and loved it dearly, but as one Councillor was heard to mutter glumly, "I was not the little lady that my mother was...." I returned to the Cardiff office with relief and was congratulated by my superiors for having done a good job (even Mr. Armer, who was never lavish in his praise, admitted this).

The only real distress in the department after my return from Carmarthen was in the Finance Section. According to the rigid rules on expenses laid down by the Government, staff expenses diminished weekly when an officer was away on work. As I had been in Carmarthen for six weeks, I learned from a worried Finance Officer that I would get only 2/6d for my final week at the Bear!

I was amused at his consternation and urgent advice to appeal for special consideration to cover the real cost, and explained that I was glad to meet this small financial deprivation as part of my war effort. In fact I often felt guilty at earning a good salary when so many people of my age were far less well paid and had much more tedious work to do in return.

A large proportion of my time as a Regional Welfare Officer was spent in advising Local Authorities when they encountered unusually difficult billeting problems. Once while I was in west Wales I was asked to visit a mining town outside Swansea to enquire into the pros and cons of a Welsh couple's application to adopt their little London evacuee. Legal adoption was at that time a rather haphazard affair, often conducted by solicitors.

I wrote to the couple to arrange a visit and then went to the town to seek them out. All the terraced houses looked much alike and I asked someone in the street where Raymond T, the little London boy, was living. I was met with blank astonishment until I gave the name of the would-be adopters. With relief the neighbour said, "Oh, you do mean Sonny Owen," and directed me to a house a few doors away.

Like most of the town's inhabitants at this time, Mr. and Mrs. Owen spoke only Welsh in their home. Not surprisingly, Sonny, at nearly four spoke nothing else. He and his mother had left London when he was a baby and both had been billeted on the Owens, but Sonny's mother had soon returned to the City, leaving her baby in their very kindly hands.

The Owens had no other children and now looked upon Sonny as their son. They were a friendly likeable couple and obviously devoted to the little boy, whose best interest, I thought, would be to remain in Welsh Wales. Fortunately the Owens were able to give me the mother's address in London, and I wrote at once to my sister, Marjorie, to ask her to consult the young woman about the proposed adoption.

Very shortly I had a written report from Marjorie that the mother's consent was readily given, and Sonny's legal adoption by the Owens went ahead. I have often wondered how it turned out, but like so many of my encounters with other people's children it was not my business to follow things through to the end. I could only wish them all well and go on my way.

Whenever possible my friend Alice Carroll and I would travel together in her ancient car to do our various jobs in west Wales. In 1944 I was often concerned with the reception of newly arrived evacuees, while Carroll would go off to sort out all sorts of problems over the care of maladjusted children. It was never easy to find hotels or lodgings in the remote areas, but we always got in somewhere and would spend the evenings together.

I never enjoyed observing the reception arrangements for unaccompanied children on their arrival by train. Often tired and tearful, they would be taken to a bare hall to wait for some strangers to collect them, after looking them over in a way that was all to reminiscent of a market place.

75

On one awful occasion I found that certain children had been labelled with an 'H'. This was to indicate that they were bed-wetters and should be accommodated in a hostel. Before long there was uproar in the hall as well-meaning but over-zealous volunteers tried to separate brothers and sisters, if one had the ominous 'H' and the brothers or sisters had not. No doubt their parents last injunction had been for the children to stay together at all costs.

My duty was simply to observe and report, but when attempts were made by force to separate the screaming children I simply could not stand it, and using what authority I had, I declared that the brothers and sisters should not be separated. After promising to take full responsibility for my high-handed decision, the wretched labels were ignored, though the matter was fully reported to the Powers That Be by the disgruntled voluntary helpers.

Poor Alice Carroll had also had a tough day, and when we met in the evening in the rather dreary lodgings we had found, we were both exhausted. As if all this was not enough, we found that we had to share a double bed as there were no others. Alice persuaded me to join her in a night cap of whisky before we finally tumbled into bed.

Some hours later one of us had a call of nature, and as we had no idea where the lavatory was, I suggested to Carroll that she should fish under the bed in the hope of finding the necessary receptacle. As she did so, Carroll revealed, one by one, an entire dinner service, which had, no doubt, been put there for safekeeping. We were both reduced to hysterical giggles, though we did eventually find the lavatory before it was too late.

Next morning as we were driving to Aberystwyth we were stopped by the Police who searched the car for eggs. There was a thriving black-market in many of the rural areas, but we were not guilty. We managed to get a couple of single rooms in a hotel in Aberystwyth though the town was crowded with American soldiers on leave. As if we were never to be left in peace the Americans in our hotel got very drunk that night and noisily serenaded Carroll's neat little fur boots, which she had unwisely left outside her bedroom door under the fanciful delusion that someone would come and clean them.

I knew Carroll was rather nervous and was bound to be alarmed by the threat of an Allied invasion, so I finally shouted very crossly to the men to shut up and go away, which they did. No doubt the poor fellows were on leave before 'D' Day, but we did not know that at the time.

By the end of the year there was every hope that the war in Europe would soon be won, and I was looking ahead to the prospect of being accepted for Relief Work overseas.

When the Evacuation Service officially ended, by no means all the evacuees left the Reception Areas. Some had been virtually abandoned by their parents, others had lost their parents and their homes through the air raids. The luckier ones were soon reunited with their families in the Cities.

Long after the official scheme had ended I was sent on my last journey to Aberystwyth to report on the arrangements that had been made for the final exodus of evacuees from west Wales. Five hundred boys and girls were due to return by a special train to Liverpool. About 90 were accommodated in rest centres in the town over night, the rest were brought to the railway station by the people with whom they had been living for years. Some since 1939. Their departure was very different from their sad arrival. I have never seen such a hullaballoo as there was when the children, of all ages and sizes, swarmed into the station lugging huge suitcases not to mention various pets, while their faithful foster-parents followed after them, weighed down with further provender. The station might have been a busy market place.

I noticed rather sadly that some of the children had labels fixed to their coats, in case their parents did not recognise them. At last they were all packed into the carriages, the whistle blew and the train moved out of the station. Caps and hands were waved frantically and the strains of Welsh hymns could be heard from the carriages until the train was out of sight.

I could not help wondering about the children's reception at the end of their journey and of how much disillusion and unhappiness might lie ahead for some of them. Looking back I wondered whether the whole Evacuation Scheme had been worthwhile. It certainly saved lives but the disruption of family life that it entailed was a high cost to pay. Perhaps its most valuable feature had been to show one half of the country how the other half lived. The Haves and the Have-Nots were brought face to face for the first time in Britain.

Paid Welfare Services were employed for the first time too, to improvise new ways of helping deprived children. Problems inherent in the Evacuation Services forced the Government to employ professional Social Workers, a thing that had never happened before.

There was growing awareness of the plight of destitute children still languishing in out of date Victorian workhouses under the Poor Law system, in fact the public in general began to see the need for change.

In 1940 the Welsh Board of Health had appointed the first paid, qualified Social Worker in Wales. It would still be another eight years before new legislation showed the way for deprived children to be given a better chance in life. It seems likely that experience born of the Evacuation Service played its own part in speeding up the change.

Chapter 14
With the Save the Children Fund

Early in 1945 I was accepted as a Relief Worker by the Save the Children Fund, and was due to leave London in March that year with the first convoy of Relief Teams to go into Europe to help the war stricken civilians there.

Although this had been agreed with the Welsh Board of Health, by a stupid oversight I had not got clearance with the Ministry of Labour to leave my present job. I remain eternally grateful to the late Geraldine Aves, then Chief Inspector of the Ministry of Health, who, by dint of energy and enterprise, managed to winkle out the relevant bit of paper from the Ministry of Labour just in time for me to join the Relief Team. I still have a sneaking feeling that Miss Aves may not have been too sorry to see me go. My tendency to say what I thought, however unpalatable, had often disturbed the even tenor of Welfare Conferences in Whitehall. Even so, I remain deeply indebted to her for quick and effective action when I was most in need of it.

Apart from the Ambulance Service, no civilians had left Britain during a war since Florence Nightingale fought an epic battle to provide the armed forces with a decent medical service. The Relief Workers' concern was with the civilian population, and would ultimately be centred on the unfortunate inmates of Hitler's Displaced Persons Labour Camps.

General Montgomery had pronounced that all the Relief Work in Europe must be done under the auspices of the Red Cross, though the individual societies might work independently. Relief Workers were required to wear Army Uniform and the whole operation was subject to military regulations.

The Save the Children Team consisted of a dozen men and women, two ambulances, two lorries and a jeep, with enough equipment to make us independent as well as supplies for the work we were to do. Early in March, with the war still in progress, the first convoy of relief teams assembled in Grosvenor Square in London. Besides the Save the Children contingent, there were teams from the Quakers, (destined, though they did not know it, to be the first to reach the stricken Belsen camp) the British Red Cross, St. John's Ambulance Brigade, the International Girl Guides and Boy Scouts and the Salvation Army.

The weather was superb when the large convoy, led by a Red Cross worker in a very small car, moved slowly away to our unknown destination. We guessed that the first stop would probably be somewhere in Belgium, and the Channel crossing was safely over before our troubles began.

Our Red Cross leader, soon to be nicknamed Fast Flossie, had obviously never learned the maxim that it is necessary in a convoy to proceed at the pace of the slowest vehicle. She set off briskly and in no time had lost the rest of the convoy. The first casualty was the Girl Guides' Mobile Canteen, in which its driver in a frantic effort to 'be prepared' only succeeded in driving into a tree. No one was hurt, but this encounter left the canteen no longer mobile, and we had no alternative but to hurry on without it.

It was in late afternoon after driving all day, that we were finally hailed by a British Army Officer, who directed us to a large house standing in its own grounds, somewhere in Belgium. The house was an empty shell, and tired as we were by then, everything we needed for our maintenance had to be unpacked. I remember our frustration on finding that all of the cooking utensils had been carefully covered with grease, no doubt to preserve them from rust, which meant that everything had to be washed before we could have a meal. Of course, there was no hot water, and by the time we had somehow managed to concoct a meal and unpack our camp beds and sleeping bags, we were thankful to crawl into them.

I was delighted to find a small lake in the grounds, this served well in place of baths, as hot water was still at a premium.

It was some weeks before we had instructions from the Army to move into Holland where we were just in time to see the last train loads of our Forces moving towards their final battle front.

I wish I could describe the glorious exploits of the first Save the Children Team in Holland, but the true facts are very different.

Having been lectured and warned in London of what we would have to face in helping the plight of the 'dying', it was a complete anticlimax to find when we reached Holland, that, while the civilian population was extremely hungry and had suffered obvious hardship, they were perfectly able to cope with their own problems. In fact, there was nothing there for us to do.

It was, of course, not possible to move the Relief Teams into Germany where our help was really needed, until the war in Europe ended. In the meantime we felt bored and useless, and matters were not helped within our own team by the growing awareness that our leader and his deputy could hardly have been less suited to their jobs.

I have never found inactivity easy, and as we could hear the guns of battle quite clearly in the distance, I decided one day to take a closer look. I got on my ancient bicycle, which always travelled with me, and set off in the direction of the gun fire. After a few miles I noticed that the countryside was very bare and certainly quite deserted, but it was not until a loud explosion went off behind me, that I realised I had gone too far. Peering closely at the sparse bushes still growing around, I was alarmed to find that some of them concealed the muzzles of machine guns. I did not stop to enquire which side they were on, but pedalled back to our billet as fast as as I could.

We were billeted in S'Hertogenbosch when we heard the announcement of the end of the war in Europe on May 8th. In fact, the first intimation I had of this was the sight of an elderly Dutch woman releasing a flag from an upstairs window, crying out that there was peace with tears of emotion streaming down her face. Our final move as a team was to Den Helder, where the whole of the coast was lined with trenches and bunkers, still littered with the belongings of German soldiers, who, no doubt had left them in a hurry. The sight of their old photos and pin-up girls on the makeshift walls was immensely sad, and somehow brought home to me the utter futility and pointlessness of war.

Once I was awakened early by the slow, steady tramp of soldiers' feet and rose in time to see columns of German prisoners of war marching through Den Helder. The men bore all the marks of defeat about them. Some were so ill and exhausted that they had to be supported by their comrades. They all looked utterly down and out.

After two months enforced idleness I was glad when the news came from Save the Children Headquarters that our team was to be disbanded. The Leader and deputy returned to London, while the rest of us joined medical teams which had followed us into Holland.

I was fortunate to join a team led by Dr. Vincent Doyle, late of the Rotunda Hospital in Dublin, who had all the qualities so sadly lacking in our previous team leader. Vincent Doyle was an intelligent, engaging young man who combined humour with integrity, and who managed to imbue his large team of nurses and ambulance drivers with a sense of unity and purpose. His deputy was an excellent woman doctor from New Zealand, we were 24 in all; I was to act as the team's Welfare Officer. It included two Dutch nurses and three Swiss, the latter were quickly nicknamed the Swiss Misses, and were, I think, the most competent and hard working of the lot. The catering side was run by a very nice cook from New Zealand. Apart from Dr. Doyle and four of the ambulance drivers we were all women. Our backgrounds varied as much as our ages, though most of the nurses were young.

We all got on well, and I was infinitely amused by Daphne and Theo, late of Eaton Square, whose upper-crust demeanour and Saville Row uniforms concealed great kindness and humour. Although attached as ambulance crew, they immediately became responsible for the drinks department, which was always well stocked.

I joined the team at Delft, which was a refreshing contrast to Den Helder, with its quiet canals and charming street markets, though food was still sadly lacking. Until other needs arose, Vincent Doyle asked me to act as quartermaster, which enabled me to dole out a lot of our ample provisions to the hungry townspeople who had given us all a warm welcome.

Once a week we drove a jeep to Rotterdam to collect food supplies from a British Army depot there. The friendly NCOs always gave us generous treatment, but we learned from bitter experience to keep the canvas flaps of the jeep tightly closed, or risk losing chocolate, cigarettes and butter on the return journey.

Gangs of quite small children would be on watch at likely traffic stops in the centre of Rotterdam, and if an Army jeep slowed down, they could leap up from behind to snatch any goods within reach. It was quite uncanny how they seemed to know by instinct just where the best items were to be found.

I am sorry to say that we were driven to knocking their small hands off the back of the jeep, but like agile little monkeys, I am glad to say that they seemed to come to no harm.

It was a great pleasure to share our provisions with our Dutch friends (though not to have them snatched from us) and I well remember giving some dried fruit to an elderly woman who held it in her hands as if it were gold. No doubt she had seen none for years, and was quite unable to speak from emotion.

We set up a hospital unit in the town and were still awaiting the arrival of patients, until, on one rather foggy night the alarm was raised and our expectations with it, but we found that one of our drivers had mistaken a canal for a road and driven a jeep straight into it. The two Dutch nurses were passengers and one was knocked out in the process. Nobby Clark, the driver, dived in and quickly pulled her to the surface, the other nurse swam to the shore and all was well, but at last the hospital unit had received one casualty; the jeep was soon recovered, and so was the patient.

Our main entertainment in Delft, for again there was no work for us to do, was at the local Rowing Club, where, with their customary hospitality, the Dutch made us all honorary members. I now found myself receiving rowing instruction instead of saving the civilian population and in the process I made at least one lifelong friend with whom, I am glad to say, I am still in contact.

We heard a great deal about the privations the Dutch had suffered during the war. One evening when I was visiting a local family, I asked the hostess how her husband had managed to keep out of the German clutches for the whole period. Without a word I was shepherded upstairs to witness his instant disappearance under the bedroom floor boards. He reckoned he could do it in 60 seconds, and often had to when the house was searched.

At last we were given the go-ahead to move into Germany. Although sorry to say goodbye to our Dutch friends, we were all delighted to be on the move, and hopes were high that we would at last be able to do some useful work.

We were to take over a hospital unit that had been set up not far from Lubeck to care for sick inmates transferred there from the infamous Belsen camp. I cannot recall much

84

Compton Martin -- 1939, Fairbridge children going for a ride with Edwin, a local farmer and excellent friend.

Fairbridge children aboard the SS *Esperance Bay* --
destination Australia, 1939

All aboard -- *The Canadian Pacific*-- destination Vancouver, 1940.

Fairbridge Farm School, Vancouver Island.

Travemünde Children's Home -- 1945

Top Row - Paul Tomaschec (L), beside Dorothy Watkins, Ethel Baker (top row R) and some of the Polish children.

Camp fire at the Polish Children's Home, Travemünde, 1945.

about our journey there except the miles of wasted ruins that was all that was left of Hamburg. It seemed completely abandoned and with the stench of death in the air. Later the countryside was peaceful and beautiful, and I caught a glimpse of red squirrels in the fir trees.

When we finally reached our hospital unit, a continuous high wailing of the wretched inmates could be clearly heard from the entrance. We soon learned that all the sick Belsen patients who were well enough to travel had been sent to Sweden to be cared for there, our hospital was left to care for those with little hope of survival, and we could only help to make their last weeks or months as tolerable as possible.

Dr. Doyle took me round the wards soon after our arrival to see what help, if any, I could give. In the first ward we entered the woman patient had just died. It was to be same sad story over and over again. What I found so terrible was the youth and potential of so many of the young patients. I remember one 'teen age Hungarian girl who attempted to speak English with me, and the courage and gaiety she showed in the face of imminent death. Only seven of the sixty or seventy patients survived. Of these, two young sisters had already been laid out in the gas chamber when the Allies arrived to rescue them in the nick of time.

Chapter 15
The Polish Children's Home in Travemünde

It was only a matter of weeks before I was summoned by Dr. Doyle and told that the Save the Children Fund has been asked by UNRRA (the United Nations Relief and Rehabilitation Association) to administer a new rehabilitation centre in Travemünde for Polish children in the ten Displaced Persons' Camps in and around Lübeck. The idea was to select the most needy children and to give them a month at the seaside in the hope of building them up to face the winter. Dr. Doyle asked me to take charge of the project, which really involved acting as a go-between with the Polish who were really to run the place and the British Military side, to ensure that everything went smoothly. I was, of course, delighted to be given this opportunity and relieved that I was to be allowed to choose two members of the hospital team to help me.

I had no hesitation in asking Ethel Baker and Nobby Clark to join me. They were both ambulance drivers but were most willing to turn their hands to anything that needed to be done.

Ethel Baker had been one of the ambulance drivers in Bermondsey throughout the war and was a stalwart, cheerful young woman, with a great sense of humour and was quite unperturbed by any crises. Incidentally, it was her ambulance team in London that was later to be awarded the George Cross.

Nobby Clark was a typical Liverpool lad with an easy temperament and plenty of energy. They both agreed to join me at what soon became known as the Polish Children's Home at Travemünde, and in no time at all we had packed up our few possessions in a jeep, and were on our way.

Speed was essential, as it was hoped to receive the first batch of 200 children from the camps as soon as the two large, empty hotel buildings on the beach at Travemünde could be got ready for them. Although the place looked imposing, we soon realized that apart from beds, blankets and linen it was an empty shell. It had cooking facilities, with a rather pretentious young man as dietician in charge. I heard more from him about calories than I had ever heard in my life. The British Army provided the food and we soon found that there was a splendid supply of excellent wine in the cellars.

Polish officers, all ex-prisoners of war, were to look after the children, while a contingent of Latvian, Lithuanian and Estonian women came daily from a nearby camp to do the domestic work. Although the bathrooms and lavatories had cold water laid on, Ethel Baker and I could find no vestige of toilet paper in the place. Fortunately, we were able to rip up yards of brown paper from various packages in the building, and so provide the lavatories with this essential need.

The day after our arrival, we drove to Lübeck to meet Colonel Turner, the British Army officer who had overall charge of the ten Displaced Persons' Camps in the area. He proved to be a most friendly co-operative man, with a keen interest in, and sympathy for, the people in the camps. I felt at once that we could not have had a better man on our side.

Before the arrival of the first batch of 200 children at Travemünde, a charming nineteen year old French girl was seconded by UNRRA to help us. Nicollette was a Parisienne who had had a very hard time during the war; fortunately this had not dimmed her light-hearted approach to life, and she proved to be an ideal companion for us and for the children.

The Polish officer who was to head the whole Pied Piper operation was Paul Tomaschek, a bespectacled ex-teacher, who concealed great warmth and humour behind a serious demeanour. He spoke excellent English, which was a great bonus, as none of the other Polish officers spoke a word of it. Not even the one woman among the officers, who was always referred to as the 'she teacher', but we all managed to communicate in spite of this.

One fine day in July lorries arrived with 200 boys and girls, destined to spend a month's holiday with us. Batch after batch lined up at the entrance, where each child received a squirt of DDT powder from Nicollette as a disinfectant. (Since then DDT has fallen out of favour, but I do not think it ever had an adverse effect on our Polish children. No doubt in the camps they had become immune to most things).

The children were accompanied by a number of 'teen-age Polish girls who had grown up in the Camps, and who now acted as helpers with the little ones, some of whom were under school age. Most of the boys and girls were pale and undersized, many were barefoot and all were appallingly dressed. Even so, they were lively and cheerful with no sign at all of emotional deprivation. Those orphaned by the war had quickly been absorbed into other families. They had, too, the advantage of growing up in the country, where even the debasing lack of freedom and other privations, could not subdue the strong religious faith of a naturally devout people.

I was amazed at the aptitude shown by the Polish officers in looking after the children. The Home was run on the lines of a Scout and Guide camp, though without any of the rules or of our usual trimmings. The children were divided into about nine groups, according to their ages. Each group chose its own name, banner and leader. The older boys called themselves Gdynia. I never see or hear that name without remembering their raucous rendering of it, on all and every occasion. Among the smaller contingents we had the Sprites of the Forest, the Samaritans, Wolves and Indians among us.

I was interested to see that the total lack of toys proved no problem. The beach provided their playground and rewarded them with coloured stones and shells, to their great delight. Luckily we could also provide chalks and paper and these were a very popular choice. In short, there was never a dull moment.

We spent most of the days on the beach and in and out of the sea, while every evening there was always a glorious camp fire in the great hall, where no one thought of complaining that the fire was made of red paper. Under the superb guidance of the Polish officer, Mr. Karimcerz Craigkoska, who acted as the entertainments officer, there would be games, songs and dances until bedtime. Luckily we had a piano on which he played with professional expertise.

Mr. Craigkoska spoke no English but we all thought him an excellent fellow. I was sorry to hear later that he was suspected of having entertained the Germans with equal zeal and might ultimately be shot for it. He was a natural entertainer, and I devoutly hope that he was not.

Most of the children arrived with little more than the clothes they stood up in, and as they were to spend a month with us the most urgent problem was to find them a change of clothing, so that their own might be washed and mended. We had no children's clothing among our equipment, in fact the only things we had were enormous flannel garments called 'helpless shirts' which were presumably meant for the dead or dying.

Ethel Baker was an excellent needlewoman and we decided to cut up this material and make it into pants and tunics for the children. We managed to locate an ancient sewing machine, only to find that it possessed no needles, a frantic appeal for these to Colonel Turner met with success, and Ethel was soon busy concocting dozens of small garments.

When I told Colonel Turner that our next main problem was how to get the children's clothing washed, with no hot water, he amazed me by pointing out that a laundry was functioning in the basement of one of our buildings. It was, apparently, manned by several Hungarian prisoners of war, who were awaiting repatriation.

Ethel Baker and I climbed innumerable steps down to the bottom of the building, on opening the door we were met by a cloud of steam, through which a number of little men appeared, looking for all the world like the seven dwarfs. When one approached and the clouds of steam subsided, I saw that he was of quite normal size. He spoke no English, but luckily I remembered my one phrase of Hungarian, which I tried out tentatively on our new friend as I was not sure of its meaning. It must have been alright as it received a rapturous response, and through the international code of mime and gesture, the Hungarians agreed to wash our children's clothes weekly.

The next problem was to divide the clothing so that it could be returned clean to the rightful owners. We concocted what the East End of London would have called a Bagwash, and implored the Hungarians not to get the various bags mixed up. In no time Ethel had made enough small garments from the hated 'helpless shirts' which were calmly accepted by the children, as they must have accepted so much else in their young lives. In due course, after an urgent appeal to the SCF in London, we received reinforcements of adequate clothing for the children, which was a great help.

Following my experience in our wartime Evacuation Service, where bed wetting had been a major problem, I found it difficult to believe Mr. Tomaschek when he told me that this was not the case in our Children's Home at Travemünde. I simply could not believe him, and one morning Ethel Baker and I decided to strip all the children's beds just to check whether they were wet or dry. The Poles won the day. We found only four wet beds out of over 200. Incredibly, these children, many of whom had been born in Displaced Persons' Camps, with all the suffering and privation this involved, had somehow survived without serious emotional damage. No doubt one reason for this was that they had remained in family groups in the camps and had retained the inherent stability of country, or even peasant, stock.

I was greatly impressed by the Polish officers and their younger helpers' treatment of the children. I doubt whether any of them, with the exception of Paul Tomaschek and the 'she teacher' had ever been in charge of a large group of children before, but I never saw one raise a hand to a child in anger, nor did I witness the endless nagging which was all too familiar to me in Britain.

The atmosphere at Travemünde was very relaxed. No one fussed (except myself!) when a twelve year-old girl went missing one day. When I told Mr. Tomaschek of my concern he replied imperturbably that the child had probably gone home to one of the camps. I urged him to check this, and he agreed to do so, though obviously not convinced of the need. He proved to be right, of course, when a little later the child was found to be back, safe and sound, with her family.

Like all the health conscious British, we had organised a Sick Bay in the Home, and when one lad was found to have a rash and a very high temperature, he was admitted to the isolation of the Sick Bay. Again I was made aware that the Poles thought this unnecessarily fussy, and I had to admit defeat when we found the same evening that our invalid had inexplicably joined the rest of the children round the camp fire, one glimpse of the solitary Sick Bay seemed to have effected a miraculous cure.

When, at the end of a month's stay the time came for our first batch of children to return to the camps, we were warned to check what they took with them. Had we not done so, half the sheets, electric light bulbs and any other moveable equipment would have vanished with them. Stealing had been a necessary part of the survival of these children and we certainly could not blame them for it. We saw them off in their convoy of coaches with real regret, but with the satisfaction of knowing that their holiday had been a great success.

During the summer I was approached by Mr. Tomaschek to discuss the concern felt by the Poles about the number of Polish children in Germany who had been taken away and placed either with German foster-parents or in German Children's Homes. Their names were changed and all traces of their identity destroyed. The Poles at Travemünde were determined to rescue these children and I was invited to join a Committee that had been formed in order to do so. I readily agreed, and felt honoured to be included as the only non-Polish member.

I cannot say that I was able to be of great help as my knowledge of the Polish language was almost nil. I would sit beside Paul Tomaschek at the meetings listening as fervent and almost endless discussions went on, which he would translate to me in a whisper. Sometimes he would become too involved in an argument to translate anything, until I nudged him to ask what was going on. Too often he would simply reply "He says yes", or vice-versa. However, the Committee did succeed in transferring a couple of dozen Polish children from a German Institution.

With them I recognised sadly all the symptoms of emotional deprivation that I had become familiar with in war-time Britain in our hostels for maladjusted children. The newcomers varied in age from the very young to those in their early teens. It was only the latter who remembered their Polish names and identities and who were able to pick out the younger ones as also being Polish. I did wonder secretly whether, from affection, some little Germans may not have slipped into the group, but I would never have dared to voice any doubts on this score.

One of these boys was seriously crippled and confined to a wheelchair. Nearly all showed signs of having suffered from the worst sort of institutional treatment. Only compassion made it possible to like them. I fervently hoped that, with the flair the Poles showed in caring for children, the pathetic little group would in time overcome their inability to give or take affection and might eventually achieve some happiness in life.

During one of the short periods between the departure of one batch of children and the arrival of the next, the Poles arranged a day's outing by coach to Plon for all the helpers in the Home. It was tremendously hot, and when we finally reached our picnic place on the banks of a lake, our strongest wish was to have a bathe. No one had had the sense to bring a swim suit, but undismayed the bolder spirits among the women sidled off to the rushes after lunch, and emerged in a curious variety of scanty underclothes for a swim. Concealment was not easy, as the water was very shallow and after a short flounder we emerged to dress again as best we could.

It was typical of the Poles that one of the officers got left behind on the return journey. Once again my natural concern at the poor fellow's predicament at being faced with a 50 mile walk back to Travemünde was pooh-poohed, and the coach sailed on without him.

Travemünde was not very far from the Russian Zone and on one occasion I was asked to travel to a Russian camp with a group of refugees who wished to return there. The journey by jeep and lorry went quite smoothly until we reached the camp itself. The huge gates were heavily barred and manned by armed guards, they opened slowly to let us in, and then clanged closed ominously behind us. Irrationally I wondered with a faint tremor, whether I should ever get out again. Life size posters of Stalin dominated the camp, and I was not at all sorry when all our passengers had disembarked and the great gates opened to allow us to escape to freedom.

Dr. Doyle and the rest of the SCF hospital team kept in close touch with us at the Children's Home and Colonel Turner was always a tower of strength. Not all the British soldiers understood the Poles as well as he did. I remember one telling me that he would rather have the Germans anytime. I replied rather sharply "You know why. If you told a German soldier to shoot his grandmother, he would do so. If you said it to a Pole, he would shoot you."

On September 23rd, 1945, Colonel Turner and I were invited as guests of honour to a special luncheon at Camp P13, where a plaque was to be dedicated in honour of those who had died there. The stone plaque had been made and beautifully decorated at the camp, where it had been placed near the improvised Chapel in the grounds. It is worth noting that all the Polish Camps for Displaced Persons had made similar Chapels of their own. These simple places were very well kept and constantly used.

I must confess that my clearest memories of that grand occasion was of the seven course luncheon, accompanied by far too much wine, and the pleasant drone of endless speeches. Friendliness, good food and drink shone from all our faces. It was indeed a memorable day. I still treasure the album I was given at the end of it, complete with photographs of the plaque, the Chapel and all the hundreds of Poles at the camp.

On the 1st October that year I had, for personal reasons, to return to Britain. I left Travemünde with great regret, and was very sorry to say goodbye to all my colleagues there, both Polish and British, as well as the children. It was sad, too, to leave Vincent Doyle and the rest of the hospital team.

On my last night at Travemünde the Poles organised a splendid farewell party, when it was ended I was given another album, this time compiled by the staff and children, depicting their group emblems and drawings with lots of signatures at the end.

I was particularly moved by the dedication:- *'To the unforgettable friend of Polish children'*.

Certainly for my part, I have never forgotten them.

Chapter 16
Greece: Working for UNRRA

After a couple of rather troubled months in Britain, I heard that UNRRA wanted Welfare Officers to work in Greece. I had been replaced by the SCF at Travemünde and was free to offer my services to UNRRA, particularly as Greece had always played a special role in my family's affections. My sister, Marjorie, had spent a year there in the 1930s and my mother earned a medal from the Greek Red Cross for her work with the Greek Merchant Navy, part of which had taken refuge in South Wales during the war.

Without much ado I applied to UNRRA to work in Greece and was delighted to be accepted. My brother, Vernon, and I had always been fascinated by the country, largely through Byron's exploits there, in particular his splendid poem starting with the lines:-

'The isles of Greece, the isles of Greece,

Where burning Sappho loved and sung....'

which had always been something of an inspiration to us, and still remains so.

Just before Christmas, 1945, after countless injections against every possible illness, I made my way to London from Wales to catch a plane to Athens. I met two friendly British girls at the airport who were to join the same flight. Patty Cecil was going to Greece under the auspices of the Save the Children Fund. She was an expert in make-do-and-mend as well as being a very bright and amusing person, and her job would be to teach the Greeks how to make the most of the scanty materials they had. The other girl, Lulu Photiades, was a London Greek who had been working as a radiographer for the Ministry of Pensions. She had joined UNRRA to work in the same capacity in an Athens' hospital and was bi-lingual.

When we finally boarded an old Dakota plane which closely resembled a tram, we found, among the few passengers with us, a resplendent Naval officer covered in gold braid, and were amused to learn that he was an Admiral in the NAAFI. The flight was uneventful until we changed planes in Rome, when the weather became increasingly stormy and the pilots warned us that we were in for a rough passage to Athens. They teased us that we, as the weaker sex, would all be sick. It proved to be by far the bumpiest flight I have ever experienced, but I am glad to say that we three girls stood up to it well, though the co-pilot was sick. He told us later that he had never been on a worse flight and that several planes had crashed that day on the same route.

By this time Patty, Lulu and I were on excellent terms and we made our way together to the large UNRRA Headquarters in the centre of Athens. On arrival we felt we might well be in America as 90% of the personnel were Yanks. This was understandable so soon after the war, when few countries in Europe had many civilians to spare, and I must say that I found the Americans to be excellent workers, their only fault being a tendency to write six pages of instructions when one would have been ample.

Although it was winter, the sun shone on us and it was wonderful to be in Athens. The city was almost empty of traffic and the magnificent sight of the deserted Acropolis dominated the scene.

Patty and Lulu soon went off on their separate ways, though we all promised to keep in touch and did so, as far as circumstances allowed. I was told to stay at the Acropolis Hotel headquarters in Athens, where most of the UNRRA staff were accommodated, until I was posted to a country district. Once again I was kitted up with Khaki uniform and attended lectures on the work and problems likely to confront me.

The political situation in the country was extremely uneasy. Greece was, in fact, on the brink of civil war. I was warned against any involvement in politics and in particular to avoid showing the slightest bias to any of the numerous factions over the distribution of goods.

I found that most of the non-Greek UNRRA personnel worked in teams in the country areas, but my guardian angel must have whispered in the Chief Officer's ear that I would do better on my own! At any rate I learned with delight that I was to work from an office in Thebes where I would be responsible for the work in a large surrounding area, which included dozens of small towns and villages. My Greek assistants included two interpreters, two drivers, with a jeep and two lorries for transport.

The roads outside Athens were so pitted by holes and war damage that even the jeep could only proceed at a snail's pace. I was met in Thebes by Jack Sykes, a British SCF worker, from whom I was to take over.

The office consisted of two rooms containing only the bare essentials for living and working. Electricity and water were laid on, but there was no lavatory. This lack was supplied by the local hospital, a few doors down the street. Jack took me along and rang the huge door bell, we were soon admitted by a large hairy patient in pyjamas. I was directed to the lavatory, while Jack waited outside. It contained the normal tiled floor with two places for one's feet, and a hole in the middle, at least I found that the flush worked. Jack looked rather disappointed when I emerged unscathed, and explained that he was hoping that I would pull the wrong chain, in which case I would have had a shower.

We returned to the office, where I met my interpreter, Sterios Zervas, a young man of nice appearance and good intelligence. I learned later that his family came from Smyrna, from where they, and thousands of other Greeks, were brutally evicted by the Turks in 1922.

Although self taught, Sterios spoke very good English and was to prove himself to be an excellent colleague. My driver, Demetrious Matsagouras, was a likeable rogue, chiefly memorable for his knowledge of where the best wine was to be found in the surrounding villages. He spoke no English, but we managed to get along in German, which he had picked up during the war, when he was one of many Greeks deported to Germany to do forced labour. Somehow I feel that even the Germans would have had difficulty in getting much work out of this idle fellow. I knew nothing about driving, but the UNRRA Transport Officer in Athens warned me that in the end Matsagouras would probably wreck us all. We certainly had some narrow squeaks, but always averted absolute disaster.

I learned that the country was divided into areas, each being called a Nomus, and administered rather like our County Councils, for Local Government purposes. Our area stretched from the Gulf of Corinth to the seaport of Khalkis, on the opposite coast. It comprised about 100 villages, including 13 which had been burnt down by the Germans in retaliation for harbouring British and Colonial Service men.

The main welfare function of UNRRA was the distribution of goods, i.e. clothing, blankets and food, to the local villages, working through the equivalent of our Parish Councils, to see fair play, and, if possible, to ensure that those in greatest need had the first priority.

I would be notified by UNRRA office in Athens when supplies had been sent to a village and would arrange to visit the place as soon as possible to check on its methods of distribution. I soon got used to Sterios's warning that we should have to make an early start on the following day. This might well mean 5 a.m., if our destination was a very distant village. His knowledge of the area had been learnt when Jack Sykes had run the office, and was to prove invaluable.

With only very damaged roads going was extremely slow and dusty in our open jeep. On arrival we would nearly always find the village elders sitting inside the local Taverna, or outside in the square, if the sun was shining. Wherever they were, ouzo and portions of goat cheese were set out on a table beside them, and with the traditional Greek hospitality, Sterios and I were welcomed to the circle. I soon grew accustomed to having large bits of cheese thrust into my mouth on a fork while I was talking, though I was always wary of the ouzo, which was a rather lethal drink.

After these preliminaries I was able, through Sterios, to bring the discussion round to the question of the distribution of the UNRRA goods. Nor was it easy to persuade these old gentlemen that priority should be given to those who were in greatest need. In a country where poverty was endemic there was an ingrained tendency to reward the most successful and to treat the poorest with contempt.

Needless to say, these distributions of valuable goods in desperately short supply excited passion in the community, so much so, that some of the village councils decided to make theirs by lottery rather than risk dispute and dissatisfaction in their villages. I shall never forget the sight of an infuriated bearded old man who approached me indignantly waving a woman's bra, which was all he had received as his share of the lottery. It must be admitted that much of the clothing we received from UNRRA was totally unsuitable for use by the poor in remote Greek villages.

It was painful to find bales of women's high-heeled shoes on offer to women whose feet were two or three times larger than anything we had, and who, in any case, needed sturdy sandals for the tough terrain in which they lived. One can only hope that since then Relief Agencies have learned that raw materials are of far greater use in stricken countries than cast-off clothing, however generously donated.

Suddenly in January our expeditions to the villages were curtailed by snow. In Greece the weather never did anything by halves, and I awoke in the office in the small room that I used as a bedroom, to find over two feet of snow outside which utterly transformed the small town of Thebes and the countryside around. There was nothing to be done but to wait for the thaw.

In the meantime I had an unexpected visitor whose jeep was held up by the snow en route from Northern Greece to Athens. He was a large, genial young Englishman, accompanied by a massive Alsatian dog. I gave both a cordial welcome, though it was obvious that my accommodation was pretty limited. Luckily William had his own camp bed and bedding, but as he was very cold, I offered him the nearest thing I had to a hot bath, which was a big tin tub. We heated the water from kettles on the primus, and when all was prepared, I moved modestly into the next room while William sank thankfully into the hot tub.

This was too much for the improvised bath which immediately overflowed and soon both rooms were awash, but as the floors were simply bare boards no great harm was done. The huge dog took it all in good part. He was a very friendly well-behaved dog.

After the usual supper of bacon and eggs William told me that he had just been discharged from the Indian Army as cuts were being made prior to India's independence, and he was on his way to Athens to join UNRRA as a transport officer, for which he had already been accepted.

I was, by now, aware that some of the best laid plans did not always work out with UNRRA and I warned William that when he arrived at the UNRRA headquarters no one would know anything about him, let alone what he was to do. I said that the only definite question likely to be put to him was whether he wanted NAAFI or PX rations. I strongly advised the latter, which was the American variety and infinitely superior.

Soon the snow had gone, and with it went William and his dog. Months later I met him by chance in Athens. He told me that everything had happened exactly as I had foretold, in fact, I am sorry to say that he was never given any sort of job and returned to England later in the year.

I have no wish to decry UNRRA's work in Greece which filled a great need at the time, and which, in my case, I found to be responsible and I think effective. Unfortunately, like so many large organisations, there were some idiotic loop holes that should have been avoided.

An even worse case of waste was that of poor Lulu Photiades, who found on her arrival in Athens that what UNRRA needed was a Radio mechanic, not a Radiographer, and she, too, through no fault of her own, was never given any work and after months of idleness eventually returned to England.

As soon as the snow cleared, Sterios, the driver and I were off on our round of villages again. Usually on our visits we were quickly surrounded by a crowd of people who often confronted us with all sorts of problems. Once, in a remote mountain village, a couple of small children were produced, both having apparently been bitten by a dog suspected of having rabies.

Even the suspicion made it vital for the children to go to Athens immediately for hospital tests and injections. The village had no method of transport except by mule, even our jeep could not reach it, and we had had to make the last part of our journey on foot.

I promised to make the necessary travel arrangments at once, but was rather taken aback when a gory parcel containing the dog's head was produced, which I was asked to take to Athens for analysis. Both Sterios and my driver recoiled in horror at the idea of travelling with this object but I over-ruled their scruples, and the wretched parcel accompanied us to Athens. I am glad to say that after six weeks in a hospital in Athens, both children were cleared of infection and returned home. I was informed by UNRRA headquarters that as a precaution against rabies all the dogs in the village were to be shot, and I was asked to confirm later that this had been done.

I returned to the village with a Greek Military Officer who soon proved to be the most trigger-happy man I have ever met. On our arrival there nothing was safe. I cowered behind the jeep as he peppered everything on four legs that came into sight. I have no idea whether all the dogs were killed, and could only report to Athens that several hours shooting had taken place. For my own part I felt lucky to have returned to Thebes unscathed.

On another memorable occasion I was asked to visit a remote nomad village where a man was reported to have a bad abscess in his tooth and needed transport to the hospital in Thebes. We made our way in the jeep until the road finally petered out and then proceeded on foot over the bare hillside. We arrived at the nomad settlement after about a quarter of a mile, to be greeted by the horrendous barking of two or three really savage dogs. Sterios hurled a piece of rock at them just as they were called off by their owners and retreated, growling ominously through bared teeth. The dogs were, of course, trained to guard the sheep and goats which were the livelihood of these people. I felt sorry for any would-be thief who came too near their property.

The nomads spent the summer with their flocks in the mountains, returning to their primitive villages for the winter. Their round mud huts were roughly thatched, with only a hole in the centre to release the smoke from their open fires.

I was invited into one, where a number of men and women were sitting on a raised mud seat around the fire. The place was so dark and full of smoke that I was glad to get out. The poor fellow with the abscess, his face swathed in bandages, was obviously in pain, and I was glad to deposit him at the hospital after a long, bumpy journey back to Thebes.

It is fifty years since I made that journey, and I believe in that time these mud huts have been replaced by something less primitive. Certainly I had never seen anything like them in the rest of Europe, in fact they would not have seemed out of place in the wilds of Africa.

Life in Greece never lacked variety. Our area was extensive and the villages scattered and remote. Once, while the days were still short, our driver lost his way, and the jeep got stuck in deep mud in the back of beyond. It was already getting dark, and when Sterios and our driver, Demetrious, failed to move it an inch, we decided to make our way on foot to the nearest village to ask for help.

It must have been about 8.30 p.m. and pitch dark when we found one in complete darkness, as everyone in it had already gone to bed. We soon roused the inhabitants and told them of our plight. In no time a group of a dozen or more cheerful men, plus two mules, were making their way with us to the jeep, lit by a lantern and with one man carrying what looked like a blunderbuss, we might have been a raucous hunting party.

At last we reached the jeep, the mules were harnessed and roped to the vehicle, urged on by shouts of encouragement and much brandishing of sticks, the poor beasts did their best to shift it. Not an inch would it budge, and while I was wondering what could be done next, the men removed the mules and placed themselves around the jeep. I could hardly believe my eyes when with a shout of "Ho-la" they lifted it out of the mud and on to safer ground.

I am glad to say that each man was promised a pair of boots before we went on our way. This was the first of many instances which showed me how extremely effectively Greek men could work when they had to, though well able to do just the reverse when they had the chance. It was another proof, too, of their inherent good will towards people in difficulty, as many British and Colonial servicemen found when things went badly wrong for them in the last war.

It was still winter when I was asked by UNRRA to visit the prison in Thebes and report on the conditions there. Until then I had not known of its existence, but I soon found the building in the precinct of the town, and made my way there, accompanied as usual by Sterios. Nothing could have been less like an English prison. The building itself was unremarkable if rather dreary. The usual high walls and great locked gates were much like any other prison, but there the resemblance ended.

The Governor was cordial and allowed us absolute freedom to look around, and through Sterios, to talk to the prisoners. The accommodation consisted of a number of large, bare rooms on the ground floor. The atmosphere was cheerful and relaxed, in spite of the almost total lack of comfort or amenities. I found that 90% of all the men (there was no women's prison) were political offenders. There seemed to be no practise of segregation, and when I asked, in a room which accommodated about 30 men, how they managed for food, they showed me a primitive sort of Army stove, where they cooked their own meals. The whole place had the atmosphere of an Army camp rather than a prison. The warders seemed to treat their charges almost paternally, though I have no doubt that the relationship could have changed in an instant to deep hostility if given the cause.

It was still very cold, and there was no heating except from the one stove. Several men were lying on the floor and were obviously pretty ill. I asked the men if they could do with some more blankets and clothing, and the offer was accepted with enthusiasm. The Governor readily agreed to send a batch of prisoners with us to collect the stuff from our local store in the town. We were accompanied by an armed warder, but I was both alarmed and amused when he handed his gun to a prisoner, while he locked the gates behind us as we left.

I thought I might see a mass exodus at this point, but the gun was returned to the warder and the mission was accomplished without further incident. I was glad to know that these friendly, likeable fellows would be a bit warmer for the rest of the winter. My period in Greece coincided with a lull between the civil wars which tore the country apart in the mid '40's.

I sent a long report to the Chief UNRRA Officer in Athens pointing out the very real hardships in the prison, which included a total lack of medical amenities. I had seen one man said to be dying of T.B. simply lying on the floor in a corner of the room with all the others. At the same time the lasting impression I was left with was of the cheerful, invincible spirit of the prisoners. I suspected that it arose from the fact that they were living together with none of the sterile isolation which poisoned the atmosphere of our British prisons.

In March the spring arrived without warning, and the hillsides around Thebes were covered with the most beautiful wild flowers of every description. I remember Sterios arriving at the office one morning with a glorious branch of apricot blossom, which he presented to me. The Greeks I met seemed to have a natural appreciation of their country's beauty.

Their religion, too, played a very real part in their lives; Easter was the climax of their year. On Good Friday the large church in Thebes was crowded by day and night while the ceremony of the Passion of Christ was enacted, accompanied by the devout intoning of prayers by the Priest and congregation. On the following night a long procession lit by candles made its way through the town, ending in and around the church for the final midnight Mass.

Shortly before 12 the Bishop, in his glorious flowing robes and tea cosy hat emerged from the church flanked on each side by a small chorister, each carrying an enormous candle to illuminate the Bible, balanced precariously on an improvised lectern, from which the Bishop read the last lesson. On the first stroke of midnight from the church clock, all the bells in Thebes rang out. Numerous shots were fired to scare away any evil spirits, while with cries of 'Allelulia' and 'Christ is risen' people in the crowd kissed each other and went home rejoicing.

Sterios had invited me to breakfast with his family. The meal consisted of coloured hard-boiled eggs and Retsina.

Then came the great ceremony of the roasting of a lamb on a spit in the courtyard. This took four hours (though it seemed longer). It was the custom for neighbours to call on each other during this waiting period, and for the host to offer his visitors slices of especial delicacies on a fork. In fact the entire Easter Sunday was spent in feasting and rejoicing, greatly assisted by unlimited wine.

Quite apart from its very real religious significance, I found it typical of the Greeks either to starve or eat well. when I tried to explain the rationing system in Britain during the war, with our weekly egg, etc. I was simply laughed to scorn. I met no one in Greece who ate fewer than three eggs at a time, if they were not available they would simply go without. I was amused, too, to find that most Greeks would consume a big bunch of grapes in an instant, while a cucumber would disappear like a banana, skin and all.

It was an Easter that I shall never forget, and which brought home to me as perhaps nothing else would have done, what a vibrant, living thing their religion was to the Greeks. For the first time I really felt a part of Greek life and identified with it.

Even so, life was full of surprises, certainly the most incongruous task I was given by UNRRA was to officiate over the distribution of typres in Thebes. I have always disliked cars and at that time I could not even drive, in fact it would have been difficult to find anyone less suited to this task, but mine was not to reason why, etc. etc. The great day duly arrived and I awoke to find a crowd of anxious supplicants making their way to the large square where the distribution was due to take place.

In those turbulent times when everything was in short supply the value of a tyre was above rubies. The object of the distribution was to put more vehicles on the road and to ease the appalling shortage of transport. A ruling had been given that only owners of a car or a van already equipped with three sound tyres would be entitled to receive one.

Lists had already been prepared by the appropriate Greek officials of licensed car owners who would qualify for consideration. I was studying these with Sterios before we made a start when a Military Officer sidled up to me to say that the army would offer me help in case of need! Apparently there had been a riot at the last distribution which had only been quelled with the soldiers' intervention. I asked Sterios to thank the officer but to say that his help would not be needed.

There was indeed a very large crowd in the square before us when the names of successful applicants were called out and each man came forward eagerly to collect his prize. It was a slow process and it was late afternoon before we had exhausted our lists with only a few tyres still left to distribute. I told Sterios to ask the small crowd still remaining whether any of them felt entitled to a tyre, even though their names were not on our lists.

Immediately, a grey-haired old man at the back quavered out that he was in that position, he was followed by several more, all of whom claimed to have a vehicle with three good tyres. It had been a long day, but if justice was to be done it was clear that we must see all these cars to check whether they, in fact conformed to UNRRA's ruling. Daylight was fading as I climbed into the jeep, accompanied by Sterios and a Greek official, to drive to the various places in the neighbourhood where these last half-dozen cars were kept.

The whole expedition was hilarious. We found a car outside the house of each applicant. The first we examined was lying in long grass in an orchard, and had no engine. The owner's explanation was that he kept it in the kitchen, in case of thieves.

At the second place even I could see that the vehicle had no wheels, when this was queried the owner said he had lent his wheels to a friend, so that he might also put in a claim for a tyre. And so it went on, by the time we had made our last visit the moon was up, there had been just enough tyres to go round, and I felt that the ingenuity of these late applicants merited a reward, even if their honesty was suspect.

At least we had avoided a riot. In fact the whole proceedings had gone without a hitch, though whether justice was done, was quite another matter.

Chapter 17
Levadhia and Delphi

Shortly after the momentous event of the tyre distribution I was asked by my Chief Officer in Athens to take over the neighbouring area north of Thebes, where the UNRRA office was in the town of Levadhia. I gathered that certain difficulties had arisen there which needed sorting out rather urgently, so I made my way at once to Levadhia. When I arrived there I was astonished to find that the British UNRRA Officer who had previously been in charge was in prison! I learned that this likeable young man had let his left wing political sympathies lead him into an indiscretion over the distribution of UNRRA goods. His real mistake had been to employ a Communist interpreter, who had used her influence to give political bias to UNRRA's work at a time when it was obviously wrong to do so.

Accompanied by Sterios I went straight to the Mayor to try to persuade him to free poor Harold, whose worst fault was probably gullibility. After about four hours of negotiations, we were successful, though only on the understanding that the unfortunate prisoner would leave Greece immediately, on his release. It was hardly a propitious start to my stay in Levadhia, but better was to come.

While I was still wondering where I could find to sleep, I was introduced to a splendid resident who said at once that I could have a room in her house. Her name was Kathryn Kahli. Her husband was a medical consultant who had a private clinic in the town.

Both were educated, charming people who, from the start, treated me like a favourite daughter. Through them I probably learned more about Greece and Greek living than from anyone else. I remained in contact with Kathryn long after I had left Greece until she died in old age in 1989.

I found the Levadhia office was well-equipped, with an additional interpreter, Jim, a young Greek, with excellent English and an intense ambition to emigrate to America, which was shared by a number of other young Greek men at that time. I came across many older men who had returned home after working in the United States for years. The poverty of their own country had driven them out, but in the end their homesickness and love of it had brought them home again. I now had to divide my time between the two areas around Levadhia and Thebes, with a drive of about thirty miles between each office.

As summer arrived I spent long days visiting the scattered villages in both areas. I soon found that an early start was essential, as all work stopped at noon in the hot weather, and usually restarted at about 4 p.m. The appalling state of the roads slowed even the jeep down to a snail's pace and we were soon coated with dust on our endless drives to remote villages.

If the work, by happy chance, took us within reach of the coast we would picnic and swim during the heat of the day. I taught Sterios and my driver, Demetrious, to swim though at first they were too shy to bathe anywhere near me. Later in the afternoon work would restart in the nearest village, and it was often dark by the time we got back to either office.

If the trips were too far for us to get back the same day, we would take sleeping bags and spend the nights under the stars. This was no hardship in the glorious Greek weather, though on one occasion when I had chosen to sleep on a beach, I awoke to find the sea lapping round the end of my sleeping bag and a crowd of villagers gazing at me with amazement from the top of the little cliff above the bay. Determined not to appear abashed as I felt, I rose, shook the water from the sleeping bag, and made my way back to the jeep as if it was the most normal thing in the world. No doubt there was talk in the village later of the mad habits of foreigners.

During the weekends I had frequent treats and excursions with Kathryn Kahli. I shall always remember my first visit to Delphi, that marvellous place, then unpolluted by tourists, with only the mists and presiding mountains, still haunted by the gods and goddesses which invoked the prophecies of the past. It was while we were driving on the road to Delphi that I suddenly realized we were passing through Arakhova, an amazing town clinging to the mountainside facing the towering heights of Parnassus.

My brother, Vernon, had told me that one of his school friends, David Cochrane, the nephew of the British Ambassador in Athens, had spent the summer holidays of 1929 at the Embassy. He was nineteen years old and his sudden disappearance in Greece caused great alarm, as it was feared he had been abducted, and the whole affair suddenly assumed political significance.

Search parties scoured the mountains until, after six weeks, David's body was found on the slopes of Parnassus. It was clear that he had been climbing alone and had fallen. Vernon had told me that David was slightly lame after an attack of polio as a child.

I knew that the main search had been based on Arakhova and as we approached the town I asked Kathryn to stop there to see whether anyone recalled the affair. After some enquiries we met the local schoolmaster, who took us to his house where he led us onto a verandah which looked straight across at Parnassus. As he opened the windows wide he suddenly shouted 'Pou inez, Cochrane?' (Where are you Cochrane?) which for six weeks had re-echoed through the mountains as the search party that he, himself, had led scoured the countryside.

I wrote to Vernon about this encounter. As a result he wrote a beautiful poem called 'Arakhova and the Daeman', which was later published in 1948 in his third book of verse. The schoolmaster told me that ever since his death the place where David fell was named Cochrane's Point, so at least the poor fellow achieved a sort of immortality.

111

According to Vernon, he was highly gifted. Astonishingly, Vernon had received a postcard from David which must have been sent off the day before he disappeared.

Another weekend outing was to Itea, then a small fishing village on the Gulf of Corinth, and not the fashionable seaside resort that it is today. Kathryn Kahli included me in an invitation she had received to attend a Christening there. On a gloriously hot summer morning we piled into a lorry with a crowd of other friends to make the long drive to the coast. As usual in Greece several of the young men came armed with bazoukis, and music and singing accompanied us all the way.

We arrived at Itea to find everything prepared on the beach for the Christening, with three long trestle tables loaded with food and drink for a lavish lunch after the ceremony. A font had been improvised and soon the baby was brought to the Bishop, who was a splendid figure, dressed in his full regalia, though very sensibly he wore a white overall to protect his clothing from the oil and water in which the baby was immersed. A crowd of about fifty guests watched the proceedings. I waited apprehensively in case of an accident and could not help thinking that even a Rugby player might quail at handling a wet and oily ball.

At last all the quite complicated ritual was completed and I was surprised to see a number of young men dash from the service, calling out the name of the child. They soon rejoined the congregation with the baby's mother, who I learned, was only permitted to be present after her child had been named.

By now we were all ready for lunch which was served beside the warm, inviting sea. Several of us had brought swimming things and before long we were in and out of the water. I cannot imagine a more delightful way to celebrate a religious occasion and felt sure the child would thrive after such an auspicious start. This was not the only Christening I attended in Greece, but the second was of a very different nature.

An assignment of clothing and blankets from UNRRA arrived at the Thebes office destined for one of the poorest and most remote villages in the area. It was in fact, one of several settlements made by the Greek Government for refugees from Smyrna, after the brutal exodus forced on them by the Turks in 1922. Faced with the sudden arrival of large numbers of penniless refugees, the Greek Government had little alternative but to place them in mountain settlements with the bare minimum of essentials with which to scrape a living. Many of the refugees had been well placed in Smyrna, but had been forced to leave without any of their possessions. It was only due to their grit and determination that they somehow managed to survive at all.

After a very long drive to the foot of the mountains, with a fully loaded lorry and jeep, it became clear that we would have to make the rest of the way on foot. After a fairly stiff climb we reached the village, only to find the whole place totally deserted. It was not long before we found the whole population squeezed into a very small church, where a Christening was proceeding. Without ado, we were invited in and watched the baby girl who was eventually given the name of Seraphina.

After the service Sterios explained that we needed volunteers to carry the UNRRA goods back to the village. This news was received with delight and only stopping to change from their best clothes, all the villagers raced down the hillside at a terrific speed, though one girl halted momentarily to thrust a live rabbit into my arms as a gift.

Clutching this creature to me, I am not sure which of us was the more startled, but at last we reached the vehicles, the boods were unloaded and carried back to the village with many expressions of gratitude and goodwill. I was left contemplating the rabbit to our mutual dismay. Sterios and the driver had no compunction in suggesting the poor creature should be cooked and eaten. I never found any Greek who was sentimental over animals. However, I named the rabbit Seraphina, irrespective of sex, and persuaded a nice Greek girl whom I knew to accept her on a fostering basis, only to hear later that the animal had absconded after burrowing its way out of the garden. I only hope the baby had a less eventful future.

I was not able, under UNRRA's policy, to give any gifts to individual applicants though from time to time people came to the office to ask for help. On one occasion I was told that a man who said that he and his family were in need of food and clothing was one of the Greeks who had given shelter for years to a British soldier during the war, at very great personal risk to himself. After hearing that he was still in touch with his British friend, now safely back in London, I told Sterios to ask him if he would allow me to write to his English friend to see if he could send some things out to him - a small return for saving him from the Germans, I thought. It was no good, the Greek applicant was quite willing to beg from UNRRA but was outraged at the idea of begging from his friend. This was by no means the only instance of Greek selfless generosity.

Among the hundred or so villages in my area, thirteen had been entirely destroyed by the Germans, because Allied Servicemen on the run had found shelter in them. The Greek Government was too poor to do more than finance the repair of one room per family.

It was typical of Greek hospitality that on a visit to one such family I was offered their only room for the night, while, unbeknown to me the whole family slept out under the stars. This was just another instance of the innate kindness and generosity of these country people, who, in spite of real poverty and deprivation, never once asked me for any return.

It was on our return from one of these trips that a blood-stained gesticulating figure came tearing down the hillside, shrieking for help. When we stopped the jeep, the poor fellow collapsed into it. Sterios thought that his throat had been cut, but I doubted whether he could have made such a noise had that been so. He had been badly beaten up and while we dived into our first-aid kit and did what we could for him, Sterios heard the man's story. It seems that his brother had seduced a girl in the neighbourhood and that her brother had gone to his home to revenge her honour. Unfortunately for our victim the seducer was out, whereupon the girl's brother fell upon him and gave him a thorough beating. On our arrival at Thebes we left our battered passenger at the hospital. I have often wondered whether the girl's family honour was then satisfied or if a vendetta continued until the real malefactor got his deserts.

The great event of the summer was to be a camp in the mountains for under-nourished school children, financed by UNRRA but organised and fun by Greek Officials in the area. The choice of a suitable site was the first problem. I was invited to join several day-long expeditions both by mule and on foot, before the right place was finally decided upon. The first choice proved to be so remote and inaccessible that even the Greeks finally decided against it. A camp for 200 children could hardly be set up on a site of impenetrable inaccessibility. The second choice would have been splendid, had it not already been taken over for the use of T.B. patients, whose tents were scattered all over the hillside.

On the third attempt the perfect setting was found. It lay in the saddle of low hills and distant mountains, and was flat enough to accommodate all the tents and marquees that were required. Much hard work went into setting up the camp. With the usual British insistence on the provision of lavatories for the children's use. I quite forgot to remind the Greeks to erect canvas shelters around them for privacy. At my final inspection I was amused to find a long row of lavatories in the centre of the camp, with no protection of any sort.

At last the camp was ready for the first batch of 150 boys and girls. I arrived there on their first evening just before supper time, to be met by the perplexed helpers who asked

115

me how to cook dried eggs. I have never been noted for any domestic virtues and had, in fact, no idea of what to do.

However, as dried eggs were definitely on the evening menu, I put a brave face on it, and between us we produced enough edible scrambled eggs to satisfy our customers. Although malnutrition and T.B. were endemic in Greece at that time, it was not easy to persuade the Greeks to appreciate the nutritional value of dried milk either, which was often used to whiten their cottage walls.

Tinned food was also treated with great suspicion and any tins that had got slightly battered in transit would be un-hesitatingly discarded. I tried in vain to persuade them that what British children had thrived on should also be good for the Greeks. They much preferred fresh food, and who can blame them?

Later that evening I made the rounds of the children's sleeping quarters. Each tent contained about 40 boys and girls who lay on the ground wrapped in brilliantly striped blankets. I was faintly taken aback to find the sexes mixed, teen-aged boys and girls interspersed among the little ones. I did ask gently whether there would be any advantage in arranging separate sleeping quarters for the older children, but was told at once that the children were sleeping in family groups, as they did at home, and would not like to be separated. They certainly looked serene enough, and I left with a clear picture of hundreds of shining eyes peering out at me from the bright mosaic of coloured blankets.

Towards the end of the summer new instructions came from the UNRRA headquarters in Athens, preparatory to its withdrawing from field work in Greece. It was time to hand over to our Greek colleagues responsibility for assessing and meeting the needs of the poorest of their population.

I was fortunate to have the help of Heracles Toumarous, a young solicitor who spoke excellent English, in the Levadhia office. He was both intelligent and concerned about

116

the work, which involved compiling statistics in the area, with the help of the local officials. Until then there had been little attempt to differentiate between those who were poor and those who were destitute. I little thought that it would not be long before Greece was plunged into the horrors of civil war, for a further unhappy period.

By now I was so identified with Greece that it came as a great shock to me when, in September, 1946, I was told that UNRRA was withdrawing all its welfare workers from Greece, and that my job there was finished. After handing over my work to Heracles, I said a sad farewell to Dr. and Kathryn Kahli, and to my faithful Greek colleagues who had worked so well with me and returned to Athens with very great regret.

I was soon on my way home to Wales, with much to remember of what was probably the most interesting and rewarding year of my life. Apart from my admiration and liking for the Greek people, I had found the marvellous countryside and coastline entirely to my taste. It had been an unforgettable experience to see the Acropolis, Sunion and Delphi in their solitary splendour. No wonder my spirits were low when the plane bound for Britain carried me away.

Chapter 18
Child care in Pembrokeshire

Once again back in Wales I was delighted to find my parents well. They had moved to Cardiff at the end of the war and were comfortably installed in a small flat in Roath Park. My father was glad to return to the area where he had been born and spent all his early years, though my mother and I both found it harder to relate to life in a large town.

I needed to find another job as soon as possible, especially as I was greeted on my return to Britain by a large, unwelcome Income Tax demand which I could not hope to meet until I earned some money. To add to the gloom, the autumn brought six weeks of solid rain, which after months of serene sunshine in Greece I found most depressing.

However, the prospect of work with deprived children in Britain had been greatly increased by the expectation of new welfare legislation which was then currently being debated in Parliament.

The brutal death of a foster-child in public care in 1944 had scandalised the general public. In a letter to the Times, Miss Myra Curtis, (later to be made a Dame), demanded a Government Inquiry into the care of all children deprived of a normal home life in Britain. Largely as a result of this letter and subsequent correspondence which showed widespread concern over the matter, the Government appointed a Committee of Inquiry in 1945 with Miss Curtis as its Chairman. A year later a report had been completed which recommended far reaching changes in the care of deprived children in this country.

Until then responsibility had been divided between three different departments of a Local Authority, namely, Health, the Education Committee and the Public Assistance Committee. The Curtis Report, as it came to be known, recommended the setting up of a single Children's Committee in each Local Authority, which would be responsible for the care of the deprived children in its area. These would include the destitute, the delinquent as well as the supervision of children fostered privately. It was recommended that The Committee should be served by a Children's Officer as its Chief Officer, with responsibility for organising the work of the department and of presenting regular reports to the Local Authority Children's Committee.

A further recommendation was that foster-home care was to be preferred to any type of residential provision. This was understandable in view of the deplorable standards of institutional care found by the Curtis Committee in the majority of Children's Homes that its members had visited. In particular the report urged the need for more imaginative care for small destitute children many of whom were still being cared for in nursery units attached to the old workhouses.

No doubt the preference for fostering as a means of providing a child with a substitute home reflected the relative success of the war-time Evacuation Scheme in doing just this.

Although most Local Authorities made no change in their arrangements for deprived children until July, 1948, when the recommendations of the Curtis Report were largely incorporated into a new Children's Act, a few new appointments were made in 1947 by County or City Councils anxious to improve the lot of children in their care, and, perhaps mindful of future difficulties in attracting suitable applicants for senior appointments as soon as the new Act came into force.

Pembrokshire was one County Council to jump the gun, so to speak, by advertising late in 1946 for a Boarding Out Officer, whose main duty would be to find foster-homes for children then in residential care in the County. I had greatly enjoyed working in Wales during the war, and Pembrokeshire with its wild sea coast seemed almost the next best thing to Greece.

119

I applied for the post without delay, and was soon called to Haverfordwest for an interview. All went well until I was asked if I held a driving licence, I was able to say that I had, but did not add that I really could not drive. I had, in fact, been given a few driving lessons by a friend, and had sometimes taken the wheel of our jeep in the lonely Greek countryside, but I had never owned a car, nor had I had to pass a driving test as I had held my first licence before 1928. I knew I could rely on my father to help me to buy a second-hand car and it never occurred to me to refuse the job when it was offered to me, just because I would have to teach myself to drive.

My kind father, who knew no more about cars than I did, helped me to buy an ancient second-hand Rover. It was a splendid, square four-seater, which looked like a hearse and was just about as speedy.

Fortunately for me, a young friend of mine, Eira Lewis, had just been appointed as Assistant Organiser to the Land Army in Pembrokeshire. Her headquarters were also in Haverfordwest, and we soon arranged to share a very small house at Little Haven, right on the coast and within easy reach of our work places. It was really Eira who taught me to drive, and with her help I steered myself precariously through the worst winter snow the County had seen for years. There were snow drifts of up to 12 feet, and it is well known that there are seventeen hills between Haverford-west and St. David's, I have no doubt that I skidded up and down most of them.

Nor were my working conditions at all easy. I shared an office and a part-time clerk with a Probation Officer, though I was nominally on the staff of the Director of Education I was, in fact, left very much to my own devices. My chief responsibility was to find foster-homes for as many as possible of the 150 boys and girls in the Council's Children's Homes. I was also required to act as Probation and After LCare Officer for girls as well as Borstal After Care when-ever the need arose. All this for 350 pounds a year!

The work was an immediate challenge and I loved the County, so I soon set about devising a plan of campaign. It was not long before I realised that nearly all the Children's Homes staff were totally opposed to the idea of fostering.

I had no responsibility for the management or staffing of the Homes and in spite of my best efforts I could do little to win the children's confidence while the people in control showed such hostility towards me. With one exception all the Homes were still part of the Public Assistance Work-houses. Fortunately one small, excellently run Home had been administered by the Education Department as an Evacuation Hostel and the charming woman in charge gave me every co-operation in finding foster-homes for the children there.

As no boarding out had previously been done in peace time in the County, I thought it best to advertise for suitable foster-parents, and was soon driving perilously all over Pembrokeshire to follow up subsequent enquiries. I was heartened to find a reassuring warmth and friendliness among the country people, a number had already given homes to wartime evacuees and were very willing to foster local children when their need was made known.

It was far more difficult to reassure the children in the residential homes of all that a good foster home had to offer, particularly as most of the staff opposed the very idea that the children in their charge would be better off elsewhere. When a vacancy arose for a matron in one of the least enlightened Children's Homes, I wrote to my old friend, Ethel Baker, who had been such a tower of strength in the SCF Home in Travemünde, to beg her to apply for the post.

Ethel had been taken ill in Germany and had had to return home, so by a miracle she was not employed, though fully recovered, and though I warned her of the very poor conditions in the Pembrokeshire Home, she accepted the challenge and was soon appointed in charge. This was an enormous help to me as I now had a fully co-operative worker in what I had almost come to look upon as the enemy camp. Only Ethel's grit and humour enabled her to struggle on in her aim to improve the standards of care for the children in her charge.

Nearly fifty years later I still recall with a shudder those awful workhouse walls and the unhappiness which was so often to be found within them. Another unexpected difficulty was in my relationship with my Committee. I had for years been used to a great degree of independence and responsibility in my work, and was taken aback to find that the members were reluctant to give me a free rein, and some, who were closely involved with the various Children's Homes could not accept the need for change.

Looking back, I can see that my own failings also contributed to this lack of understanding. I was impatient of what seemed to me to be Victorian standards of child care, and did not make allowances for the very real concern some of the older members felt about the upheaval and unhappiness of the Home's staff as the wind of change blew in. In spite of all the problems I greatly enjoyed the variety of the work, illumined as it always was, by the glories of the Pembrokeshire coast and countryside.

At last the snow melted and the winter changed to spring. Whenever we were free to do so, Eira and I would drive off in her jeep to explore the coast, and, later on, the islands. Ramsay Island became my favourite place. The very friendly farmer who owned it then would let us camp in his barn, and in fine weather Eira and I would lie on the top of the high cliffs, staring down at the seals below us. Once, at low tide we explored a huge cave on the Island and had gone a long way into it in eerie darkness when we were startled out of our lives by the appearance of an enormous seal who tore past us at a speed to reach the sea. No doubt the fright was mutual, but after that we never explored the caves in depth.

We once joined an RSPB expedition to Grassholm to ring young gannets. As we approached the Island by motor launch we could see that it was totally covered with these brilliantly white, graceful birds. The noise was deafening and the smell almost equally penetrating. Many of the young birds had reached the stage when they were covered with white fluff from head to toe, and presented a prim, almost Victorian appearance.

The sky was full of hovering, swooping parents, who in all that dense crowd of birds, unerringly selected and fed their own offspring. The ringing was soon completed, and we returned to the mainland in perfect weather, which is essential in these dangerous waters.

The little house I shared with Eira was uncomfortably cramped and when I heard in the spring that an old coast-guard's hut at Little Haven was available for rent, I moved in there on my own for the rest of the summer. The hut was strongly built of stone, which was just as well, as it stood out on a rocky headland just outside the village, with the waves breaking nearly all around it. It was primitive in the extreme, though there was an indoor stove and an outside lavatory. Luckily the St. Bride's Hotel was no distance away and the two friendly girls who ran it made me very welcome for baths and dinner as often as I liked. Otherwise I enjoyed a simple life, with a bed, chair and table as my only furniture and a splendid Aladdin lamp for light.

Luckily in 1947 there was a glorious summer, both Eira and I were keen swimmers and made full use of the sea around us. We particularly enjoyed bathing at night, when the phosphorescence turned the warm water silver and our splashing created miniature fire work displays as tiny silver stars fell all around us.

It was not always calm and I shall never forget standing out on the headland in a terrible storm, wondering how any ship could survive it. I learned with horror on the following day that the Mumbles life-boat and her entire crew had been lost that night in an heroic attempt to save another ship's crew.

Work, in the meantime, had more than filled my days. Fostering arrangements had gone well ahead, with a good

123

proportion of the children in care happily placed, though mistakes and misjudgment naturally occurred from time to time. I cannot honestly recall being responsible for many girls on probation in Pembrokeshire, though one or two ex-Borstal girls used to liven my days quite a lot.

Unfortunately my relationship with my Committee never achieved the mutual friendly trust so vital to the smooth running of the Social Services. My Chairman, whom I will call Mrs. X clearly had no confidence in me and formed the habit of checking up on my work, to the extent of visiting foster-homes without letting me know, in a way that I found intolerable.

Things came to a head one day when the Chairman arrived in my office with yet another query about something I had done, or not done, and without further discussion I wrote out my resignation on a slip of paper, handed it to Mrs. X and told her to get out of my office.

I know that I should feel ashamed of this action, but I must confess that I have never regretted it. Much as I loved Pembrokeshire and enjoyed my work, I simply could not cope with the underlying sense of mistrust that lay between my Chairman and myself.

I explained this later to the very nice Clerk of the Council, when he made every effort to dissuade me from leaving. It was sad to give up after only a year's work, but I knew my own limitations and felt that no good would come of a longer stay.

Chapter 19
Cornwall...The Children's Act 1948

My parents gave me their usual warm welcome at the little Cardiff flat, while I pondered my next move. I now felt wary of working for another Local Authority and decided to return to Gower, where my brother and his wife were living on the Pennard Cliffs with a growing young family.

A woman friend of ours who lived nearby had a fine herd of goats which I had often admired, and when she suddenly found herself short-handed as her goat-herd had had to take sick leave, I offered my services voluntarily until her return. This was gladly accepted and for the next six weeks I cared for goats instead of children, and found them almost equally individual and amusing.

I would arrive early every morning at my neighbours to lead the most sedate members of the herd onto the cliffs where they would spend the day in perfect freedom, until, in the evening, I would go out to collect them to bring them home for milking and the night. Invariably at about 5 o'clock they would be waiting for me, and I really found them most patient and obliging unless, by mistake, I tried to steer a goat into the wrong stall, this was always bitterly resented and I was soon made aware of my error. I used to call my particular charges the sixth form girls and I never tired of watching them munching the tips of gorse or striking theatrical poses on the cliff tops. Sometimes, when something upset them and they champed and sneered, I seemed to catch a fleeting resemblance to the more hostile of the Pembrokeshire committee members, but my relationship with the goats was much more friendly and relaxed.

In July, 1948, the new Children's Act became law. Parliament had accepted all the main recommendations of the *Curtis Committee Report* and the way was open for a new era in child care. County Councils and County Boroughs were faced with the responsibility for appointing a

Childrens' Committee and a Childrens' Officer who between them had to find staff to run the new service. This was by no means easy.

Apart from an acute shortage of trained Social Workers, Local Authorities had in 1948 to cope with further legislation, including the demise of the Public Assistance Departments and a new National Insurance Act. The 1944 Education Act was still hardly over its teething problems.

Although the post of Children's Officer was open to both sexes, the Curtis Report had indicated that it rather favoured the appointment of a woman for the job. The prospect of a woman chief officer appalled most Local Authorities, but there was little alternative as, except in the Probation Service, men had not yet entered the field of professional Social Work.

In spite of my reservations regarding working for a Local Authority, my interest in Child Care was too strong for me to hold back from the prospect of taking part in the working of this new Children's Charter, and I soon set about applying for a post as Children's Officer in any of the areas that attracted me. These were advertised freely in the appropriate periodicals. I was not alone in finding the challenge of the new legislation exciting and very soon a large number of the best posts were filled by women far better qualified than myself. Nearly all applicants were female, a number of whom had previously worked in Local Education Departments. Others, like myself, had gained experience in the war-time Evacuation Service, while a few had teaching or nursing qualifications.

The Government Department responsible for over-seeing the Children's Service was the Home Office, which had the right to veto the appointment of any applicant for the post of Children's Officer who was thought to be unsuitable. I applied unsuccessfully for several posts, but was offered a rather interesting one by a voluntary society which I was on the verge of accepting when I received a very unexpected telegram from the Cornwall County Council asking me to attend an impending interview for the post of Children's Officer within the next week.

I was on holiday in Pembrokeshire in August, 1948, with my old friend, Elizabeth Yeo, when the telegram was sent on to me. The prospect of interrupting my holiday for a 13 hour train journey and a job I might not want, or even be offered, nearly put me off. Elizabeth almost pushed me onto the train at St. Davids, exhorting me to remember Cornwall's superb coastline and all the seals and sea birds to be found there. I little thought when I embarked on the long journey to Truro that I would spend the rest of my life in the unknown county of Cornwall.

I arrived in Truro the evening before my interview and spent the night in a rather dreary hotel. My only previous knowledge of the City was through an early novel of Hugh Walpole's but I was too tired to do any exploring that night. When I reached County Hall the following morning, I found that two other women applicants had arrived before me.

At last my turn came to confront the Appointments Committee which was mostly composed of men in rather funereal clothing seated around the large Council Chamber. The interview was conducted by the Clerk to the Council though a number of questions were shot at me from all over the room. I felt surprisingly at ease as I was by no means certain that I wanted the job and was determined that, if offered it, I would make my own terms. I was less concerned about salary than the conditions of employment, in particular how much freedom I would be allowed in directing the work of the new Children's Service. In due course I was invited to raise any points that I wished to make and had no hesitation in saying just that. I added that I knew from experience that I worked best when given a fairly free hand and would this be the case in Cornwall? Immediately a burly figure in the back of the hall rose to say that "What Miss Watkins wants to know is will she be the boss or the Committee?" This was so exactly true that I could only laugh and say no more. I learned later that the shrewd speaker was the late Colonel Edward Bolitho, then Chairman of the Cornwall County Council.

In spite of my outspoken interview I was not really surprised to be offered the job, my two rival applicants had had no relevant experience in Child Care, and the Council was, no doubt, desperate to make an appointment, as the Children's Act was now law and until the post of Children's Officer was filled very little could be done to set up the new service. Without more ado I accepted the offer and agreed to start work in Truro a month later.

I returned hot foot to Wales, where my parents were delighted with the news that I was to work in Cornwall. My father had always been interested in the County and looked upon the Cornish as Celtic relations, just as he did the Bretons. He and my mother looked forward to visiting Cornwall in the following year.

In the meantime, I had to find another car as the dear old Rover had finally given up the ghost. This time my father and I chose a second-hand open Hillman Minx which looked much smarter than the other but was rather less reliable. I had almost run out of cash after some months without employment and once again my dear father paid for the car.

When the time came I had no alternative but to return to the hotel in Truro until I could find somewhere else to live. On September 20th, I made my way to County Hall and told the Committee Clerk, whom I had met at interview, that I would like to see the Clerk of the Council. "Well, he doesn't want to see you!" was the quick reply, which though no doubt intended as a joke, had an ominous ring of truth about it. Our subsequent meeting confirmed my worst fears. Though not treated as a hostile witness I began to feel like one. Worst of all, the Children's Service was to be a section of the Clerk's Department, so that I was not on a par with other chief Officers employed by the Council, and though I did not crave any particular status for myself, the inevitable result was that the Children's Section, as it was to be called, would rank as Cinderella among the other council Departments.

As for Office accommodation, I found two junior clerks installed in a small hut in the County Hall Car Park. They were surrounded by hundreds of files piled up on the desks and on the floor. These proved to be the records of children in the Council's care passed over to me from the Public Assistance Committee, (now defunct) and the Education Department. A smaller pile from the County Medical Officer related to children fostered privately in the county whose supervision had, until the new Act, been the responsibility of the Health Department.

Looking back I can hardly imagine how I got started on the unenviable task of sorting out this human jigsaw puzzle at all. Although there were over 500 children of under seventeen years of age who had become the responsibility of the new Children's Committee, there were no coherent lists of their names and addresses, just a jumble of files on the floor. Even more alarming was the total absence of any child care staff to undertake the supervision of over one hundred children in foster homes in the County.

The four Boarding Out Officers, as they were then called, previously employed by the Education Committee had all left to take up new appointments. While the Clerk advertised for staff, I decided to approach the County Nursing Officer, to ask for her help in arranging the supervision of the foster children through the Health Visitors. The late Miss Ann White, who was then in charge of Cornwall's Nursing Services, readily agreed to this, and our subsequent warm friendship forged an invaluable link between our two services. Her deputy, Mary Witting, also became a close friend.

The Children's Committee comprised about forty men and women including a number who had been co-opted as representatives of local organisations in Cornwall that had a particular interest in child care. The Chairman was the

129

late Lady Carew Pole, who naturally eyed me with a good deal of suspicion, but who later proved to be a very good intelligent Chairman as well as a particularly charming person.

The first meeting went off well. I found the members interested and sympathetic. The co-opted members added a great deal by their lively and informed concern about the work, and I was sorry, when, in later years, the practice of including them on Council Committees was dropped.

Some of the Committee's early decisions make astonishing reading today. In 1949, the pocket money for children in care was as follows:-

Aged 5 - 8, 6d a week

Aged 8 - 11, 1/- a week

Aged 11 - 14, 1/6d a week

Aged 14 - 15, 2/- a week

Aged 15 & over (if still at school) 3/- a week

Young people in employment were allowed to keep 5 to 10 shillings a week according to age, the rest of their wages went towards their keep.

I worked early and late to get the children's records into some sort of order, only stopping to visit the Children's Homes. apart from three Evacuation Hostels which were handed over to the County Council after the war, there were eight children's Homes previously run by the Public Assistance Committee for children of school age, while those of under three were cared for in the nursery wings of four of the large workhouses, soon to be transformed into hospitals or abandoned altogether. All these places were widely scattered over Cornwall.

I soon realised that I must find myself a quiet haven in which to live. Hotel life did not suit me at all and I needed the solace of the sea beside me. At my first glance at the advertisements in a copy of the West Briton, the main local newspaper in West Cornwall, I spotted an advert for a creek-side cottage within five miles of Truro, to be let furnished.

I went post-haste to the agents, only to be told that the previous tenant had mislaid the keys and that it was not possible to look over it. In no way abashed I asked for the address, explaining that I was more interested in the cottage's situation than its interior. I think the agent was so taken aback at this that he gave me the address without demur.

I soon found the small stone cottage at Point, a tiny village beside the beautiful Restronguet Creek, which lies between Truro and Falmouth. It was just what I wanted.

I peered through the windows, but was chiefly interested in the little garden, perched high above the water, but with steps leading down to its edge. By good fortune, the owner, the late Mr. C. F. Scott lived in the village, and we soon reached an agreement that I could rent the cottage on a monthly basis for the princely sum of two pounds a week, furnished. I was installed there within a few days, and though it had no mod cons and few domestic conveniences, I was charmed with the peace around it and the ever changing aspect of the creek.

The move made all the difference to me. I really needed to escape from the problems and anxieties inherent in setting up a new department and my tiny home exactly filled the bill. The following summer I was delighted to welcome my parents for a visit to Cornwall. I little knew then that it would be my Father's only trip to the County. Less than a year later he died unexpectedly, while undergoing a minor operation. Although the cause was a tragedy, and his loss was irreparable, it did mean that the following year my mother came to share my little cottage with me.

Every winter she would travel to London to look after my sister in her small flat in the East End for a month or two, but for the rest of her long life she happily made her home with me. My mother's lively interest in my work, her unstoppable vitality and friendly disposition were an enormous support to me, and indeed to many of the children in care and to the staff, particularly those in the Children's Homes, which she visited with me regularly.

One of the first of the new Child Care staff to be appointed in the first of the new Child Care staff to be appointed in the county was my old friend and colleague, Ethel Baker. Gradually three more women joined the staff to take over the boarding out and foster home supervision. Perhaps my luckiest break of all was the appointment of Mrs. Doreen Stein as my Administrative Assistant. This involved taking charge of the indoor staff as well as being at my beck and call every moment of the day. I know now that I made intolerable demands on this intelligent and selfless woman, whose friendship and loyalty over the twenty-five years in which we worked together I shall never forget. Luckily, we are still able to meet, and as soon as do so the passage of time disappears and we talk and laugh as we always used to.

The Home Office Regional Inspectorate for the South West was centred on Cardiff, as it also covered the whole of south Wales. I soon found a fund of knowledge in the visiting inspectors which I greatly valued, cut off as I was in a rather remote rural area. Perhaps the greatest help I had from the Home Office in the early days came from the late Miss D. Rosling, then assistant to Mr. John Ross, head of the Children's Department Inspectorate in Whitehall. It was she who advised me to allow each of the Boarding Out Officers a specified area in the County with an office and a clerk, and responsibility for every aspect of the child care work in her own particular area.

As a result of this plan, these workers became well known in their own vicinity and could plan and get on with their work without interference. It was also of valuable assistance to the general public, who knew to whom to take their problems.

Gradually the child Care Service began to take shape. As new staff were appointed we rapidly outgrew the small hut in the car park and our first move was to a much larger Nissen hut at the far end of Strangways Terrace in Truro. I liked the view of the City below us, which could be glimpsed through the canopy of a large copper beech tree which stood beside it.

In 1949, just as I was beginning to feel a little more able to cope, the first real crisis burst on us out of the blue. The matron, (and sole owner) of a private residential nursery in Truro suddenly became ill with cancer and died within a week. I was notified that there were a dozen children under the age of five in immediate need of care. On enquiry I found that several of the children's parents were abroad, none of whom had appointed a guardian in this country. One boy of nine had been legally adopted by the Matron, and proceedings were in process for her to adopt another toddler. There were no resident staff. I arranged for a member of our own Homes to move into the nursery temporarily to take charge, while frantic telegrams and cables were sent off from my office to alert the parents and relatives of their children's plight.

Foster homes were found for those whose parents were abroad, and a friendly neighbour took in the adopted boy and the little one whose adoption had not been finally legalised. I was thankful when friends and relatives arrived to collect most of the children, and to get cabled permission from the parents abroad to make provision for the others. The nursery was finally closed and I could breathe again. I even got a gorgeous bouquet of flowers from one grateful parent.

The next urgent need in 1949 was to find alternative accommodation for all the tiny, destitute children still living in the old workhouses. These buildings were now in process of adaptation for hospital or other use, in any case it is hard to imagine a more unsuitable environment for small children. Apart from the gloom of these gaunt, Victorian buildings, the babies and toddlers in the nursery wings were largely in the care of the mentally handicapped women inmates.

Most of the children had been born in the workhouses and abandoned soon after birth. Many mothers were single women who had little alternative help available. War-time conditions had made a bad situation worse. It was not unusual for a pregnant girl to move into Cornwall, give birth to a child in a workhouse, and then disappear without trace leaving her baby behind her.

I advised the Children's Committee to buy two houses, each with accommodation for 12 babies and toddlers, in order to set them up as nurseries for the destitute little ones in the workhouses. Before the end of the year two suitable houses had been bought, one in Perranporth and the other in Penzance. They were soon staffed and equipped and it was a happy day for me when the last poor little workhouse waifs had moved into their new premises. I remember with what huge satisfaction I realised that this was the end of one of the worst aspects of the old Poor Law, and hoping, with incurable optimism that the worst of the children's troubles were over.

Chapter 20
Institutional care

It was time to turn attention to the County Council's Childrens' Homes. The eight scattered Children's Homes were in the charge of Housemothers but directly managed by the masters and matrons of the workhouses, who controlled all expenditure and provided food and clothing for the children in the Homes. I felt strongly that the Houseparents who were entrusted with the full guidance of the children'a lives should also be given the lesser responsibility of buying their food and clothing.

The Committee members discussed this proposal and finally agreed to the change, though some expressed doubts as to whether it would work. I am glad to say that the Homes' staff greatly appreciated their new independence, and accepted their added responsibilities with scrupulous care and good sense.

Nearly all the Housemothers had worked in the Children's Homes for years and showed the utmost devotion to the children in their care. Two large Homes catered for boys only, the three Evacuation Hostels were mixed, and the rest only accommodated girls. I was horrified to find that under the Public Assistance Department families of destitute children had inevitably been split, the boys going to one Home and the girls to another.

Gradually this was all changed and all but two of the Homes catered for mixed sexes. The two exceptions became hostels for older children. The new regime meant that at least children who had lost their own parents were not separated from their brothers or sisters.

Another difficulty was that the Public Assistance Committee had ruled that children in its care over whom the Council had assumed parental rights should have no contact with their parents or relatives until they reached the age of eighteen. The committee had also been opposed to fostering, with the result that nearly all the destitute children in the County spent their young lives in Children's Homes and had to rely entirely on the staff for care and affection. In only one Home did I find this totally lacking. On visiting this place I sensed at once that all was not well, and when I enquired from the Master and Matron of the local workhouse about the children's care, they confessed some unease about the Housemother's suitability.

The Home catered for twelve boys, and I learned that one of them had recently appeared before a Juvenile Court for attempting to harm the woman by putting some noxious substance in her tea! I must say that as I learned more of the regime in the Home, I had some sympathy for him.

I had no hesitation in consulting the county Council's Establishment Section about the need to get rid of this one unsuitable member of staff. Although the Children's Act was a good opportunity to make staff changes, I found great reluctance in the Clerk's Department to end this woman's employment. Finally I simply said that I could not accept responsibility for the children in the Home unless there was a change of staff. There was no answer to this, so I got my way. I am glad to say that the new Housemother soon provided the boys with a much happier, relaxed regime.

No sooner had I finished rejoicing over the removal of all the babies and toddlers from the workhouses than I found that a little hydracephalic girl, aged seven, was still accommodated in an old ladies' ward in Lamellion House in Liskeard. This old workhouse was in process of becoming part of the hospital system. I learned from the very nice Master and Matron there that this child, Valerie, had actually been born there, and that her mother had abandoned her soon after her birth.

Valeries was very much disabled by her large head and was paralysed from the waist down and confined to a wheelchair. In spite of this the child was bright and attractive. When I visited her I was amazed to find how Valerie had adapted herself to the old ladies ward in which she lived. Even her tone of voice and mannerisms might well have been those of an elderly invalid, except that she exuded happiness and well being, and was obviously the centre of much love and devotion from the staff as well as the inmates. In particular the Master and Matron, who had no children of their own, simply adored the child.

I made a full report of these unusual circumstances to my Committee and strongly recommended that Valerie should remain in what was virtually her home, where she was greatly loved and very contented. I did arrange for her to have some part-time lessons, as I felt it would be an asset if she learned to read. Far from missing the company of other children it seems that Valerie could not bear them. Rightly or wrongly I left her care to those who had known her from birth at Lamellion House, with my Committee's full approval.

When the next Home Office Inspector came to Cornwall, I told him of Valerie's situation. He was naturally rather shocked by the idea of a small girl growing up in an old people's ward. I asked him to visit Valerie and judge for himself the pros and cons of moving her. He returned to tell me after his visit that he thought it would be very wrong to disturb the child. I visited Valerie regularly for the rest of her short life. When she died, at the age of eleven, the whole of Liskeard mourned her loss. Even the Mayor turned out for her funeral.

It was over a year after my arrival in Cornwall that I discovered that two other destitute and abandoned children were still accommodated in what was then a large T.B. hospital in West Cornwall. Both these boys had been treated for T.B. of the bone, and were permanently crippled, though well able to get about. No one seemed to be aware in the hospital that they were also suffering equally from emotional deprivation, with no outside contacts of any kind.

By this time we had converted one of the Evacuation Hostels in Newquay into a Reception Home, so both boys were able to move there from hospital without delay. Unlike Valerie, who had been surrounded by love and care since her birth, in spite of her bizarre surroundings, our two T.B. sufferers were as wild as monkeys and seemed unable either to give or receive affection, nor could they conform to normal patterns of behaviour. The younger boy, who was only six years old, never really recovered from his early deprivations.

It was not only sick children who suffered in this way. On going through the old Public Assistance records I found that two teenage Cornish boys had been sent to a training school in Oxfordshire the previous year. Nothing more seemed to be known of them and I made a point of visiting the place as soon as I could.

When I arrived I found my two boys very keen to leave there and was not surprised at this, as it seemed depressingly like a version of Dotheby Hall, and to serve as a dumping ground for growing lads with nowhere else to go. I promised the two boys that I would get them back to Cornwall for Christmas, and they accepted this cheerfully. Both were prepared to do farm work and it was not long before they were suitably settled in jobs in this County. I should add that within a relatively short time the Oxfordshire Training Home came under new management and provided excellent help and training for lads in need.

Not long after my return from Oxfordshire, I was surprised to get a letter from one of the Training Home's staff asking whether I could help another Cornish boy, Peter, aged seventeen, who had apparently been placed there years earlier and had no contacts of any sort outside the Training Home.

A further search through the Public Assistance records revealed that this unfortunate boy had indeed been sent to the home at the age of fourteen. Illegitimate and abandoned by his mother in Cornwall soon after his birth, Peter had been placed with a private foster mother in West Cornwall, with no further contact with his mother, who had left the County.

At the age of nine he had appeared before a Juvenile Court for the theft of a fountain pen and had been sent to an Approved School in Devon. No one had apparently tried to locate Peter's mother, or relatives, and when it was time for him to leave the school, he was placed in an adult men's wing of the Redruth workhouse, until a local Councillor protested about this unsuitable arrangement and the un-fortunate boy was then moved to the Oxfordshire Training Home.

I was placed in a quandary about how to help Peter. At seventeen he was, in fact, outside the age limit to be re-ceived into care by the Children's Committee and with the Public Assistance Department no longer in existence he was literally nobody's child. After explaining the situation to the Children's Committee it was agreed that Peter should return to Cornwall and be found a farm job as soon as possible. Again I was reminded of Dickens as Peter might well have played the part of poor Smike of Dotheby Hall, who was equally without friends or relations.

In spite of all our efforts, and his own, Peter never fully recovered from his early deprivation. He spent years search-ing for the mother who had abandoned him. When he finally traced her, she had another family and did not want to know. With all his good and likeable qualities poor Peter was just not one of the lucky ones.

The five hundred children in the Council's care could be divided into three categories; destitute children with little hope of being re-established with their parents; those who were in short-term care through the temporary breakdown of the family, usually through the mother's illness and those committed to the Council's care through the Juvenile Courts, usually as in need of care and protection. Among the children in long term care were a number of war time evacuees who had remained in Cornwall due to the desertion or death of their parents.

In the next ten years all our efforts went into finding foster-homes for the children in care. We soon found that there was no shortage of people prepared to offer a temporary or a permanent home to babies and toddlers, and that the little ones blossomed with loving individual care. When, in 1952, the World Health Organisation published a report by Dr. John Bowlby entitled 'Maternal Care and Mental Health' which roundly condemned residential provision for babies and small children, our efforts were redoubled, so that it was not very long before our nurseries were converted for the use of older children for whom it was far less easy to find homes.

The effect all over the country of Dr. Bowlby's Report was really quite remarkable. Not only was residential care for babies known to be the most expensive but we were now told that it did more harm than good. For the first time, we were made to realise that only a mother or a substitute mother could meet a small child's need for individual love and care. As a direct result of the Bowlby Report, residential nurseries soon ceased to be in Great Britain as alternative methods of care took their place.

At the same time we found that the needs of slightly older children were by no means so easily met. A number of the boys and girls in Cornwall had been in institutional care since birth and our efforts to fit them into foster homes were mostly unsuccessful. Would-be foster parents either yearned for a tiny baby or for a dear little girl of under seven. Large boys or awkward girls were not in demand. Our efforts to link these older children in the Homes with their relatives were often equally unsuccessful. Too many years had gone by, and I could see few opportunities for these children to fulfil their real potential.

It must be remembered that in the early 1950s there were very limited openings for unskilled boys and girls when they reached employment age. Farm labouring for the boys and under-paid shop work or domestic service for the girls were still the norm.

After much though I suggested tentatively to the Children's Committee that we might send a few carefully selected children to one of the Fairbridge Farm Schools in Australia. I found, rather to my surprise, that Cornwall had a long traditional link with Australia through adult emigration in the last century, when poverty and lack of opportunity had driven many men to look overseas in the hope of a better future. The Children's Committee accepted my suggestion without demur, though I doubt whether I would even have made the proposal had I not had personal knowledge of the Farm Schools and been mightily impressed by the cheerful well being of the children in them.

From the first I had made a point of getting to know all the children in our own Homes, so it was not difficult to discuss the whole project of emigration to a Farm School with them. I was quite clear in my own mind that only those who were good mixers and sufficiently tough to hold their own in a large community should be finally selected. Another criterion was that the potential migrant should be without any close family ties in Cornwall. Finally, I discussed all the pros and cons of emigration with the small group of boys and girls who seemed to me most likely to benefit from the wider horizons overseas.

Not unnaturally all the children leapt at the chance of this new adventure, several whom I had not selected approached me personally to ask to be included. I did my best to point out the snags, but made very little impression.

Eventually three small groups of Cornish children emigrated to Australia to the Fairbridge Farm Schools in New South Wales and Western Australia. I kept in touch with these boys and girls through personal correspondence and from the regular reports sent to me by the Fairbridge Society. This continued until they were all grown up, and in many cases for much longer. Not all their subsequent histories were happy ones, but the majority did exceedingly

141

well. Several returned to Cornwall for holidays in later years. It was a great joy to meet them to discuss their lives and future plans.

As these children reached adolescence their curiosity about their own roots came to the fore. I was able to answer a number of queries, even, in one case, to send a girl a photo of her mother, who had died when the child was very small. It was this girl who wrote to ask my help in tracing the mother of a young friend of hers, who was quite unknown to me, as the girl in question had been sent to Australia in infancy through another organisation outside Cornwall.

By dint of some good detective work I at last traced the mother, and was able to put the girl in touch with her. My reward was one of the most moving letters from the girl that I have ever received. She said, among other things, that I would never know what this late contact with her unknown mother had been to her.

To end this saga with a success story, Mac, born in a Cornish workhouse and abandoned by his mother at birth, had grown up in a children's Home until he was twelve years old. Bright and attractive, he had failed the 11 +, but struck me as having all the right ingredients for a really good future, given the wider opportunities overseas. He was one of the first small group of Cornish children to emigrate to the Fairbridge Farm School in Western Australia. There, Mac romped through High School and University and and qualified as a teacher. We corresponded regularly and in his mid-twenties I heard that he was planning a two year working holiday in Europe. Mac asked my advice about temporary jobs in Cornwall and I advised him to apply to be a lifeguard in Newquay the following summer. He was an excellent swimmer and a first class athlete. I was exceedingly pleased when he came to Cornwall, where he worked by day as a lifeguard and in the evening in a local pub.

We met frequently and had some long talks. Instead of a sturdy Cornish boy I was confronted by a friendly, independent young man who seemed perfectly at ease wherever he was, and who planned to travel all over Europe before returning to Australia. Among other things Mac meant to play golf on all the famous links in Scotland. We had never been able to trace his mother, but before he left England he managed to find his two brothers, who had been abandoned in Devon and had grown up in the West Country.

Before Mac left Cornwall I asked him whether he had ever regretted his emigration. After a moment's reflection he replied that he could never imagine any other life.

Times, change, and child migration is now rightly a thing of the past, but who is to say that it did not fill a need for a number of under privileged children in a different era?

Chapter 21
Deprivation and delinquency

As Childrens' Departments became well-established throughout the country, Childrens' Officers decided to form an Association which had as its aim the need to improve the welfare of deprived children and to ensure high standards of work on their behalf. The Association of Childrens' Officers was in no way a trade union. It was not concerned with the question of status or salary of its members, though it certainly offered them support, largely through the formation of Regional Branches, where members could meet quarterly to discuss mutual problems and to devise ways and means of meeting them.

This was of great value to Children's Officers like myself who were rather cut off from their colleagues, and who often felt the need to talk over varying aspects of the work while we struggled to find new methods of solving the age old problems of broken families and destitute and delinquent children.

Gradually the obsession of the 1950s in finding substitute homes for children in care switched towards the plight of their natural parents. I had only once been present at the forcible removal of children from their own home and had vowed that I would never again be involved in anything like it.

From the start in Cornwall I made it my practice to meet every child who was admitted to our Reception Centre, and to get to know as intimately as possible all the children in our Children's Homes. I became aware that most of the boys and girls I talked to were deeply concerned about their own roots, though many found great difficulty in expressing themselves.

One of the best opportunities I had of really getting to know the children was during the summer holiday camps that soon became a welcome diversion from what I inwardly felt to be the very boring life in the Children's Homes. I always tried to spend a weekend or so in the summer with the children and greatly enjoyed teaching them to swim, apart from the more vital matters of getting them to talk. Once, when one of the Homes' children were on holiday in the Scillies, a rather dull, inhibited boy took me out in a boat to explore the islands. He had been in residential care since infancy, and when I asked him whether he ever thought about his mother, he dropped the oars and blurted out "I never think of anything else". He then relapsed into his usual gloomy silence, while I, startled beyond belief, realised for the first time, how little I knew of the human suffering so often concealed beneath an awkward shield of sullen indifference.

There was no happy ending to that story. The boy's mother had died in a psychiatric hospital, and all our efforts failed to make up for this loss. I doubt, in fact, whether he ever got over it.

A curious dichotomy of the 1950s was the strict division between children who were labelled as deprived, and those, appearing before a Juvenile Court for crimes of varying magnitude, who were classified as delinquent. My own findings were often very different. Some of the deprived children in care were anti-social and resorted to crime whenever the opportunity arose, while the so-called delinquents often had appalling histories of real deprivation.

I soon found that my reluctance to see punishment as a constructive alternative led me into some difficulties both in the Juvenile Courts and with my colleagues in the Probation Service. I earned the derisive title of 'Prisoner's Friend' from the Probation Officers, as my antipathy to the Approved School system became known. Though for the most part I admired and liked the staff in these schools, I questioned the wisdom of committing a possibly disturbed and deprived child to the sort of regime they offered, particularly as the outcome of these sentences was ultimately

145

to tip the unfortunate boy or girl back into the very home environment that had palpably failed to meet his or her needs in the first place.

The family history of so many young offenders proved beyond a shadow of doubt that the root of their problems lay in parental failure of one sort or another. The mother who came to a Juvenile Court when her child was in trouble and who told the Magistrate that she had given him everything he wanted, seemed unaware that a lack of proper guidance and control would inevitably lead to mischief.

Similarly, some dirty, neglected children had not been deprived of parental love and their removal from home as in need of care and protection often did more harm than good. Both intuitively and later from experience I learned to distrust labels of any sort for human beings.

As James Joyce makes one of his characters say, after being subjected to a tirade of platitudes: "I am afriad of these long words which make people so unhappy...."

The ultimate silliness seemed to me to commit naughty girls to Approved Schools. Most of these places were then a poor imitation of girls' boarding schools, with boring school uniform and team games which signally failed to appeal to, or help, adolescent girls, some of whom had already made a living on the streets. At best some girls tolerated a period in an Approved School but immediately discarded the hated uniform when they left, and with it most of the standards that the school had tried to teach them. Those who failed to conform simply ran away, and if they showed aggression or a real hostility when picked up, the result might be committal to Borstal.

Although so many Magistrates who presided over the Juvenile Courts were excellent people who tried very hard to come to the right decision in their rulings, it never seemed to me that a court of any sort was the appropriate place in which to deal with children, many of whom were in profound difficulties.

The setting up of Detention Centres for boys whom the Magistrate thought needed a short, sharp lesson also proved a failure. These centres aimed at providing discipline and strenuous physical activity for adolescent boys, in the vain hope of curing their shortcomings, while ignoring deep-rooted difficulties which so often lay beneath the surface. It was unrealistic to expect to alter a boy's bad attitudes in a short period, and many left the Centres quite unchanged, except that mixing with some who were far more criminally sophisticated than themselves made them a good deal worse and led to such a high failure rate that eventually all the Detention Centres were closed. I soon found that the common denominator in young offenders seemed to be their own deep feeling of inadequacy. This was often well disguised by a pose of arrogance and wild behaviour while immaturity and insecurity lay below the surface.

In spite of my doubts, the difficulty of controlling girls who were habitual absconders, both from their own home and from ours, led to one or two Cornish girls who were inveterate absconders being committed to an Approved School. Pauline was a case in point.

Illegitimate and abandoned by her mother in infancy, by the age of twelve no foster home or Children's Home could hold her. Reluctantly, I agreed to her being brought before a Juvenile Court as beyond control, with the inevitable result that she was committed to an Approved School, some distance away from Cornwall.

Unfortunately, Pauline continued to run away. In spite of everything our relationship remained friendly and we corresponded regularly. In one letter she wrote, 'I am determined not to run away again. I am in the school choir, we are learning to sing "Oh, for the wings of a dove...."' However, her absconding continued, even worse Pauline became violent when picked up and returned to school and before long the wretched girl was again brought before the magistrates and this time was committed to Borstal.

147

I had tried several times to arrange for her to return to Cornwall, on the basis that we could hardly do worse than the school, but things had got quite beyond my control, and it soon became clear that Pauline was doing no better in Borstal than she had before. I was horrified to learn, when she was nearly twenty, that after a further appearance in Court, Pauline had been sent to Rampton. As she was neither a criminal nor mad I did everything I could to obtain. her release. I was unsuccessful, but in spite of this really awful story I am glad to say that it had a happy ending.

My colleague, Ethel Baker, had kept in close touch with Pauline, and we were both relieved and delighted to hear of her discharge from Rampton in her early twenties, when she was found a place to work in London. Ethel met her there and was appalled to find her a nervous wreck and a shadow of the healthy girl she had been in Cornwall. However, the kindness of the family with whom she had been given the job of mother's help, together with her own remarkable resilience, led to a very happy ending. Pauline's employer actually paid for her to spend a holiday in a hotel in Truro, where she, Ethel Baker and I had a splendid reunion.

Like most deprived children, she showed no resentment towards us for our past failures to rescue her from so many pitfalls, and I only hope that she lived happily ever after. Pauline was not the only Cornish girl of under-twenty to be sent to Rampton with no criminal record, but simply for nuisance value. I made a point of visiting the place and found it hard to imagine a more unpleasant and unsuitable environment for a young girl, or for anyone else, for that matter. I did everything in my power to get the girl released and am thankful to say that she was ultimately discharged and returned to live in Cornwall.

Another of my lasting concerns was the practise of sending young people of under 16 to prison on remand if the Magistrates felt that could not be securely held in a Children's Remand Home. I visited several Cornish boys in prison and always felt that they any alternative would be preferable. On one occasion a 15 year old boy from Cornwall was sent to the Remand Wing of Wormwood Scrubs. There were 200 young men and boys there in totally dreary and squalid surroundings. I thought the staff seemed very indifferent and uncaring. The boy I went to visit had been abandoned by his unsuitable adoptive parents and was in need of expert help and care. He certainly never found it in prison, nor in the Borstal to which he was sent later.

I was so furious at my inability to help this boy and at what seemed to me to be the shocking arrangement for the young at Wormwood Scrubs, that I went straight to the Home Office to complain about the place. I did not mince my words and was only partially soothed by the cup of tea quickly provided for me by the always tolerant Civil Service.

Later I made great efforts to arouse my colleagues in the Association of Children's Officers to the enormity of placing damaged and inadequate boys in such a grossly unsuitable environment as prison, but without much success. The practise still continued when I retired from work nearly twenty years ago, and though I am now out of touch, I suspect it still does so.

I always tried to visit all the establishments to which Cornish boys and girls were sent, and on one occasion had an opportunity to call at Grendon prison, which had not long been established as the one prison which provided psychiatric help for severely disturbed male prisoners. The building was as grimly unimaginative as most prisons, but once inside it was a different matter. The staff proved to be everything one could desire, under the splendid leadership of Dr. Gray. A case conference was at once convened to discuss the future of the unfortunate 16-year old whom I had come to visit, and I am glad to say that within a very short time he was back in Cornwall.

Chapter 22
Preventive work

Although I had ample opportunity through the Association of Children's Officers of widening my knowledge of new developments in child care, both the Homes' staff and the field workers needed new openings if they were to be kept up to date. As soon as the Central Council for Training in Child Care was set up in London I encouraged the staff to go on short refresher courses, and in some cases to undertake one of the new training courses leading to a child care qualification. I was particularly anxious that all the staff should work well together, and that those in the residential service should not feel themselves to be second-class citizens, though their pay and conditions of work were even more inadquate than those of the Boarding Out Officers.

There must have been something in the air in Cornwall that blew goodwill into the work, as friendship and loyalty were blessings without which we could not have thrived and which fortunately were never lacking in the County. Even so one could not but be aware that a good deal of overlapping with other welfare services occurred, and that some unfortunate families with multiple problems might be visited by officers from four or five different departments, sometimes quite unaware of each other and even offering directly opposite advice.

The Children's Committee accepted my suggestion that an annual two-day conference should be arranged for our own staff, which would include open invitations to the Probation Officers, the Health Visitors and Education Welfare Officers, as well as to any Juvenile County Magistrates and our own Committee Members if they wished to attend particular sessions. This was a fine way of getting people together and in particular provided an opportunity to invite some outstanding speakers to give talks on relevant social work problems which were greatly stimulating.

One of the most memorable of these was the late Miss Leila Rendell who was then Director of the Caldicott community in Kent. this was, in fact, an outstandingly good boarding school for maladjusted children of good intelligence. Through dint of her own personality and perceptive insight into disturbed children's needs, Miss Rendell made an immense contribution to their well being and was an inspiration to those of us who tried to follow in her footsteps. I always remember one of her opening remarks at a talk she gave us which was to the effect that we should all be wary of fashions in child care.

Certainly I became increasingly aware of the temptation to clutch at new methods of trying to help deprived children, i.e., boarding out, closing nurseries, substituting large for small Homes, and finally to return children to their own families under supervision, after their committal to care through a Juvenile Court.

An omission in the 1948 Children's Act prevented the Child Care Services from offering practical help to families in need in order to prevent their breakdown. There was mounting pressure from the Children's Officers Association to correct this.

By the end of the 1950s it seemed obvious that prevention was better than cure and that the law should empower Local Authorities to spend money and effort in order to prevent the breakdown of families at risk.

In 1961 I reported to the Children's Committee that a thousand requests had been received for help with children neglected in their own homes. In the same year my colleague, Mrs. Belinda Banham was asked to prepare a scheme to help what were then called 'problem families' in the County. Both the Health and Children's Committees were equally involved, and as a result of Mrs. Banham's report a number of special relief workers were appointed by the Health Committee to visit and help families in which children were deemed to be at risk. Mrs. Banham took charge of the whole project though it was nominally under

151

the direction of the Medical Officer of Health. In 1963 a new Children's Act gave Local Authorities the power to give help and guidance to such families, and a new era had begun.

Every year a large proportion of the children in Cornwall's care had been removed from home simply because the mother had fallen ill. This had never seemed to me to be a sensible procedure, and as a direct result of the new Act, the Children's Committee was able to appoint four Relief Workers whose job it was to help families in their own homes in the temporary absence of the mother. Dormobiles were provided for both mobility and as sleeping quarters for these workers, who soon earned the title of 'Flying Angels'.

Their efforts, and those of the Health Department's special workers with needy families helped to improve things in the County, though poor housing and homelessness were still a problem and the numbers of children in care continued to rise slightly. It is interesting to recall that in 1958 I had reported to the Children's Committee that the number of children in our care had dropped to 384. More than half of these had been brought before a Juvenile Court as in need of care because of sexual abuse, home conditions were in many cases described as squalid and the need for more preventive help to avoid family breakdown was stressed.

In the year 1958 I also met the late Mr. Lyward, the creator and inspiration of Finchden Manor in Kent, where he provided a unique establishment for seriously disturbed, intelligent, adolescent boys. The antithesis of an Approved School, the inmates at Finchden were allowed a relaxed and to some extent a self-governing regime, under the watchful, affectionate eye of this very remarkable man.

Two teenage boys from Cornwall who had defied help in every more conventional type of home or hostel, found sanctuary at Finchden and were greatly helped there. In his book *Mr. Lyward's Answer* he set out his theory that more maladjustment and immaturity in adolescent boys were caused by nagging or over-protective mothers than by anything else.

His regime at Finchden reflected the need such lads have to revert to early childhood in a free, relaxed atmosphere, and it was significant that no women whatsoever were employed in the place. Of course, Finchden was inspired by Mr. Lyward, whose intuitive guidance and exceptional intelligence kept fifty or so really difficult boys from running amok. Sadly, the place folded after his death and just as the dreaded onset of drugs in the 70's, which altered so much for the worse.

The following year I was summoned to the County Treasurer's Office (that wizard of a man whose magic oiled all the wheels of the County Council's affairs). He told me that it had been agreed with the Isles of Scilly Council that in future I would also act as Children's Officer for that Authority. By an Act of Parliament the Scilly Council was run independently of the Cornwall County Council and this was the first I had heard of my new responsibilities. With some amusement I asked our Treasurer at what value the Island Council was to reward my services. 'Nil', was the reply, but we both knew that it was always a delight to have an excuse to visit the Scillies; I already knew all the Islands well and quite a number of the people living there.

My duties were not onerous. When a real difficulty arose I would get a 'phone call from the very nice Clerk to the Council on St. Mary's, and if we could not sort something out over the telephone, I would fit in a visit as soon as I could. For the most part the Islanders lived in harmony, but from time to time something would go seriously amiss. However happy a rural community seems there are usually one or two disruptive families to upset the apple cart.

I grew to love the Islands and formed warm friendships there. Sadly, after my retirement from work, the terrible murder of Stephen Menheniott by his father, on St. Mary's, ironically in the area called Holy Vale, cast a lasting shadow over the Islands for me, which has never really been

153

dispelled. Although Stephen had not been in the care of my own Council nor in any way my responsibility, the Menheniott family had come from the mainland of Cornwall originally and I had been involved with them intermittently through three of their other children since 1949. Stephen's death was certainly the most tragic case I have ever known and one which I shall never forget.

Chapter 23
Pity the children

To revert to the lighter side of life in Cornwall, my day's work invariably began by reading every report on a child in care that had arrived in the morning post. In this I was ably assisted by my faithful colleague, Doreen Stein, and although much of our reading was fraught with problems, the reports were illuminated by the glorious aptness of some of the Cornish placenames; as an example one referred to an eneuretic boy whose address was Washaway, Upper Grogley. Then there was the pregnant girl at Labour-in-Vain, the elusive putative father at Knave-go-by, and the unfortunate girl whose surname was Toombs who lived at Jericho, who was brought before a Juvenile Court for attacking her mother with a poker.

In a service chiefly concerned with family breakdown and social failure I hope I may be forgiven for finding humour where I could, without the loss of compassion for the human element.

It was in the 1950's that I saw a letter in *The Times* by Mr. Alec Dickson in which he urged the idea of including a year or so of voluntary service between school and college for young people in Great Britain. He made mention of the fact that few Local Authorities seemed interested in the project or prepared to make use of these young volunteers in the Homes and Institutions they ran. I wrote at once to Mr. Dickson and in no time a number of these young men and women came to help in the Children's Homes in Cornwall for temporary periods. Of course, some were more successful than others, but all brought with them youth and freshness which brightened the often rather staid routine in the Children's Homes.

The 1960s brought even greater impetus to efforts all over the country to prevent the breakdown of families at risk and to find different means of helping children in need. In

155

Cornwall, Tony Gillespie, an extremely able Psychiatric Social Worker in the Health Department, accepted a new post of Assistant Children's Officer to take responsibility for the preventive side of the child care work in the County. His skill and enthusiasm were of immense value to our own staff and more especially to the children at risk in Cornwall.

One of these, Billy R, was aged nearly four, when I first received a very disquieting report of his home circumstances. Billy was then living with his parents and an elder brother and sister in poor circumstances in West Cornwall. His father had recently served a year in prison for injuring the child when he was under two, which left Billy permanently crippled, though he could limp around. His father returned home after his release from prison. He was a difficult and uncooperative man, who showed little insight into his children's needs. Naturally local concern was aroused and it was not long before Billy was brought before a Juvenile Court as in need of care and protection. The Magistrates made a supervision order in his respect, naming the Cornwall County Council Children's Department as the agent to carry it out.

I had, from the start, been uneasy about this crippled child being left in the care of the father who had caused his injuries. Luckily there was an excellent Child Care Officer, (the title of Boarding Out Officer had long ago been dropped), close at hand in West Cornwall, who was willing and able to visit the family frequently, and it was hoped, to win the parent's cooperation.

Billy's mother was a weak character and easily dominated by her more unstable husband. The two older children presented no problems, but it was not long before I again had very disquieting reports on Billy. Either the child was accident-prone or there were further signs of some physical abuse.

The reports on the family suggested that Mr. R could not come to terms with Billy's crippled condition and was determined to cure him through various exercises. Not

156

unnaturally this child of four failed to cooperate, which further exasperated his father. The crisis came when it was reported that Billy was badly bruised after apparently falling down the stairs. Our School Medical Officer, Dr. James, who had cooperated closely over Billy's medical condition, had no hesitation in advising me that the child had suffered abuse and should be taken back to court, with a recommendation that he be removed from home and committed to the care of the Cornwall County Council. In the meantime Billy was removed to one of our small Homes under a place of safety order.

Before the date of the Juvenile Court hearing I had an unexpected telephone call from the BBC, asking me for an interview. I learned that Mr. R had written to the BBC, complaining of being victimised by the Cornwall County Council. This complaint had been passed to Mr. Desmond Wilcox, who was in process of making a number of television documentaries based on a variety of human problems to be known as the 'Man Alive' series. Two members of his team had visited Cornwall to investigate Mr. R's complaint and had already prepared a programme on the whole matter. The R family had been visited and photographed and it was later intended to incorporate the findings of the Juvenile Court hearing into the film.

I agreed to meet the chief BBC spokesman, Mr. Alan Williamson, and a young Canadian director who was with him, though I was always most wary of any publicity involving children and I knew that the County Council would take the same attitude. When we met later in my office I explained that it was not my practise to discuss personal problems about individual children with whom I was concerned, nor did I feel it would be right to expose Billy to photographs and interviews prior to the Court Hearing.

Mr. Williamson said that the BBC would like to include the County Council's views in the film which he said would ultimately be shown on BBC 2 in the 'Man Alive' series. He was very persuasive and I could see that he was keen to

157

make a fair portrayal of the serious problems involved in the R's family, but I was certain that the Clerk to the Council and the County Medical Officer would oppose our having any part al all in the proposed film.

We parted on very friendly terms after I had promised to consult Mr. Verger, the Clerk, and the County Medical Officer. As I expected, the answer when I did so, was in the negative. I rather regretted having to pass this decision on to Mr. Williamson and his colleague, as both men seemed really interested in Billy's problems and to have a sensitive and compassionate attitude towards the whole affair. I could only advise them to count us out and perhaps to consult the NSPCC, who might be prepared to provide the plaintiff's part in this case.

Later, at the Juvenile Court I saw that both the BBC men were present when Billy was finally committed to the care of the Cornwall County Council and returned to our small Children's Home in Perranporth. However, the BBC did not give up. I was again asked to take part in the proposed film and could only advise Mr. Williamson to make a direct approach to the Clerk of the Council. As a result of this meeting, Mr. Verger agreed to call a further joint meeting with the BBC, to be attended by the County Medical Officer, Dr. James and myself. After a long discussion it was finally decided that Dr. James and I could appear in the BBC film, providing we were allowed a preview of it, and approved the final version.

I was glad of this, as although I always distrusted publicity through the media, stone-walling by the Council with the inevitable "No comment", would have forced the BBC to portray only one side of a very complex matter. Fundamentally I have always felt that the public has a right to know what goes on behind closed Local Authority doors, and though I was sure that the BBC's bias when Mr. R's letter first reached it was very much in his favour, I was confident, after discussing the problems thoroughly with the two men, that the film version would be a fair one.

It was not long before Dr. James, Billy and I had completed our parts, the Children's Home and the matron were also included briefly in the film, and the two well-satisfied BBC representatives returned to London. Later in the year the great day arrived for Dr. Ted James and myself to go to the BBC Headquarters in London to see the film. By then we were all on the friendliest terms. On arrival at the BBC I was greeted by the film's director, Mr. Desmond Wilcox, with a kiss. He told me that I spoke written English. I could only hope that this was intended as a compliment, though I had my doubts.

After a splendid lunch we were taken to an adjacent room to see the film. It was called 'Pity the Children', and, as I had hoped, showed with compassion and sensitivity both sides of the appalling problem of how best to help a child at serious risk of abuse in his own home. I learned from the film for the first time that Billy's father was illegitimate and had himself suffered abuse at the hands of an over strict father, which proved once again how the sins of one generation may affect the next.

Dr. James and I returned to Cornwall able to give a good account of the film, which was eventually shown on BBC 2 in one of the last of the excellent 'Man Alive' series.

Not surprisingly Billy was a difficult little boy, as well as a physically damaged one. After some years in a Children's Home he was able to return to live with his own family. The unfortunate Mr. R had left home after the breakdown of the marriage, and nothing more was heard of him.

I was always nervous of any sort of publicity over children in care. We were fortunate in Cornwall in the local press reporters, who were invariably cooperative and discreet. Apart from the dreadful case of Stephen Menheniott which occurred after my retirement, I can only recall one occasion when we hit the headlines of the National Press. It was not a happy experience, though even at its worst the incongruity of the whole affair made me smile, if rather wryly.

It all arose when a young mother abandoned her small son and daughter in a caravan on a holiday beach site in Mid Cornwall. The local Child Care Officer who investigated the situation, found both children frightened and upset, with no sign of their mother, whom they said, had threatened to drown them.

Dennis and Sandra (as I will call them) were then aged 6 and 7 and apart from their distress, showed no signs of ill treatment. There was no alternative but to admit them temporarily to our Newquay Reception Home, where they soon settled quite happily. When enquiries made it clear that their mother had left the County, Dennis and Sandra were boarded out together with very nice foster parents in Cornwall.

The children gained immensely in confidence and well-being and when, several years later, their mother turned up and wished to see them, I refused her request. By this time the Cornwall County Council had taken a resolution assuming parental rights over the two children, on the grounds that their mother had abandoned them, and rightly or wrongly, I felt that their new found happiness and security might be shattered by the sudden re-appearance of their mother, whom both had seemed to fear.

Mrs. H (as I will call the mother), then made an application to the Juvenile Court to rescind the parental rights resolution and for Dennis and Sandra to be returned to her care. When the case came to court, someone had alerted the National Press and the Court Room was thronged with reporters. The County Council opposed the application, but Mrs. H's expert solicitor, the late Mr. Philip Stephens, made a most eloquent attack on the heartless refusal of the Children's Department to allow a devoted mother to see her own children. As a result, Mrs. H won the case and her children were returned to her care.

Needless to say, the reporters on the National Press made the most of the matter. The worst headlines I saw were in a very prominent daily paper and read: 'Bumbledon worse than Dickens....'

Even though I had tried to act for the best, I was rightly reproved by my Committee for not having consulted the members before refusing a parent access to her children. I never made the same mistake again.

I could not help feeling slightly vindicated when I heard from a colleague in the South of England some time later, that both children had again been abandoned by their mother and were again in Local Authority care. Mrs. H was, I think, one of a small minority of mothers whose sense of possession was stronger than her love for her children. Certainly her own well-being always came before theirs.

Needless to say, the further breakdown of this family never hit the headlines as the Juvenile Court hearing had done.

My admiration and liking for Mr. Philip Stephens was by no means diminished by his attack in the Court. In fact, he would have been my first choice as a solicitor had I ever found myself on the wrong side of the law.

Chapter 24
All change in Social Work

It was not until 1965 that the Children's Committee approved of our acting as an agency for Legal Adoption and our first Adoptions Officer was appointed that year. This meant a very serious and important addition to our child care work. Until then the placing of children for legal adoption had been largely in the hands of various voluntary agencies with the addition of babies placed privately by their parents or, quite frequently through the intervention of doctors and nurses. The arrangement had often been haphazard and I had felt for some time that the duty of providing a legal adoption agency should be part and parcel of the work of a Children's Department. Mrs. Pearl Evans was the first Adoptions Officer to be appointed by the Children's Committee in Cornwall. A trained Social Worker and ex-nurse, she was blessed with good judgment and a sympathetic personality. Both were greatly needed in this post.

As the years passed I became convinced that the choice of suitable adoptive parents needed the wisdom of Solomon if tragic mistakes were not to be made. I came to distrust the secrecy which still seems to bedevil the whole affair. No wonder that even happily placed adopted children are confused by a lack of knowledge of their own roots, while some parents see faults in their adopted children as a direct legacy from their natural mothers. After much thought I came to the conclusion that anxiety could mar the happiness of an adopted child, and that the qualities of serenity and warm affection in potential adoptive parents would provide the best hallmark for success.

Although in many ways so satisfying and constructive, I came to the conclusion that selecting adoptive parents was the most difficult and hazardous of all the jobs in the Child Care Service. However clear-cut and admirable their motives appeared to be, it was not unusual to find that some childless couples who were desperate to adopt a baby, concealed deep anxieties of their own which might mitigate against their success in this venture. Experience led me to favour young couples with children of their own, whose main wish seemed to be to offer a loving home to a baby or child who lacked one.

It would be stupid to make formal rules as to who would or would not make good adoptive parents, everything must depend on the warmth and stability of the potential applicants, having said this, I can only add that any mistake in this assessment can lead to absolute disaster for all concerned. Public concern about the growing number of small children reported as seriously abused in their own homes led to instructions from the Government that all Local Authorities should set up a register of children known to be at risk and that local case conferences must be regularly convened to decide on any necessary, action concerning them.

Cornwall was lucky in being able to appoint Dr. Voyce, the first, paediatrician in the County, to Chair our conferences, which were also attended by Dr. James, the School Medical Officer, and myself as well as the appropriate Health Visitor and Probation Officer concerned with any particular child who came up for discussion.

These informal meetings were called whenever the need arose, and were of enormous help in deciding the appropriate action when a child appeared to be at great risk at home.

They also had their humorous moments. At one meeting a telephone call interrupted the proceedings. Dr. Voyce's wife had rung to say that their youngest child had bumped his head on a fall from his high chair, and to ask whether he should be taken to the hospital for an X-ray. "Good heaven no" was the doctor's reply, "I should probably be had up for causing the injury".

Nearly twenty years after the Children's Act of 1948, dissatisfaction was growing about the number of officers of various departments in any given locality who might be concerned with the problems of a family in need of help. Cases were quoted in the press of a single family having been visited by officials from the Health, Children's and Probation Services, as well as those concerned with Education and Social Security. A family so swamped by different agencies might often receive conflicting advice which sometimes resulted in confusion worse confounded.

Pressure grew for the formation of a single Welfare Service with the aims of meeting all aspects of a family's special needs, and in particular the avoidance of much duplication of effort.

As a result of a White Paper which came before Parliament in 1965 and was entitled 'The child, the Family and the Young Offender', a committee was set up to review the organisation and responsibilities of all the relevant departments and to consider what changes were desirable to secure an effective family welfare service. The late Lord Seebohm was appointed as its Chairman.

In July, 1968 this committee's very far reaching report was published and came before Parliament. Its main recommendation was to establish a unified Social Service Department in every major Local Authority in the country.

Although this change would result in the end of the Children's Service as well as the welfare functions of the Education and Health Departments, it was not unexpected and was welcomed by the majority of Children's Officers in the hope that the result would be to the benefit of the families concerned.

It was unfortunate that this marvellous change in social work provision came just before the reorganisation of Local Authority boundaries, which, apart from badly disrupting life in the 1970's, also greatly limited the funds available for staffing and setting up the new Family Welfare Service. No one then foresaw the enormous pressures that were to be put on the new Departments nor the impossible burden they would place on the limited and often untrained staff involved.

There was also a dangerous over-simplification in the Seebohm Report in recommending that all the needs of a family should be met by a single Social Worker. It was wrongly assumed that supervision by a senior worker would be sufficient to guide inexperienced staff.

The Report's wide-ranging recommendations on training were pie in the sky when funds were not available and the pressures of day-to-day problems made it impossible to release untrained staff, however much they might wish to earn a qualification.

Altogether the new Welfare Service got off to a very difficult start, and once again Local Authorities were involved in a game of general post. The first essential was to appoint a Director of Social Services. Never before had this over-worked and under-paid profession attracted the large salaries now offered as a bait by Councils keen to attract the best applicants to fill these posts.

I suppose it was not surprising that even the most highly qualified and experienced women Social Workers were pipped at the post by men. The job was seen as an administrative one, and this seems to have been considered a masculine prerogative. Only a handful of Director's posts were given to women, the imbalance was as great as in 1948, only the other way round.

I had decided to apply for the Director's post in Cornwall, although I was then 59 and would, I was sure, be considered too old, and in any case of the wrong sex, as I was pretty sure that my Council would decide to appoint a man. At the interview that followed I was treated with utmost kindness and courtesy, but the final question as to whether I considered myself to be a Social Worker or an Administrator simply made me laugh. I replied that I was a Social Worker but that the two were not incompatible. As I expected I did not get the job, which went to Mr. E. Murphy, who had previously worked in London.

I became one of two Assistant Directors when the new family Social Services Department was set up in Cornwall. I cannot pretend that it was easy to see the Children's Department that I had helped create absorbed into the larger Family Service.

The situation was made less painful for me by the fact that I was nearing retirement when the re-organisation took place in 1970. I still continued to oversee the children's side of the work, but my main task was trying to bridge the gap between the past and the present, and to give support to the staff who had given such devoted loyalty to the Children's Department for so many years.

Although incurably optimistic, I could not help regretting that the pendulum had swung so far from women to men when it came to making senior appointments in the Social Services, and I feared that the very size of the new departments might be their own undoing.

In the past I had often been accused of keeping a crystal ball under my desk for consultation when beset by grave human problems. It is true that I relied more than most on my intuitive feelings, and often said that one could not solve human problems like algebra. Once, at a Conference, I had defined the most essential qualities needed by a Children's Officer as sound judgement, wide sympathies and imagination as well as an iron constitution. Certainly imagination was not the least of these.

Now in the sixties I welcomed my approaching retirement. I was too old to embark on all the changes needed in the new Department, though I did my best to oil the wheels as far as I could.

I had worked for the Cornwall County Council for nearly twenty five years, and felt loyalty and affection for it. I had been wonderfully well supported by my own Committee

166

and had always enjoyed very fair treatment by the whole Council. The charm of Cornwall lies not only in its remoteness and beauty, but also in the rugged individuality and kindness of the Cornish people, even though there is a danger of their being swamped by invaders from other less propitious areas.

Notable among my memories of outstanding County Council Members was the late Mrs. Charles Williams of Trengwainton, Penzance, Chairman of the Health Committee, for many years, who, with the splendid County Medical Officer, Dr. Curnow, did so much to raise medical standards in Cornwall and helped among other things to obliterate the scourge of tuberculosis in the county.

The large, imposing figure of Mrs. Williams concealed a very warm personality, in which a keen intelligence competed with an acute sense of humour. Both greatly enlivened Council meetings where her easy manner and total lack of self importance made her greatly loved.

Another memorable member of my own Committee was the late Mrs. Polly Lanyon of Falmouth. A doctor's widow, Mrs. Lanyon was invariably dressed in a black alpaca cloak, her dark dress always had a stiff white collar, and the whole rather sombre outfit was topped by a black straw boater. In spite of this grim, Victorian appearance, Polly Lanyon combined a ready wit with a most compassionate and lively interest in everything around her. Far from being archaic, her every utterance was shrewd and up-to-date.

I must admit that Polly was always my favourite Member, and when after her death the sad day came for the memorial service in her honour, I was moved to find the large Parish Church in Falmouth absolutely packed with men and women from every walk of life, who had known and loved her.

Most of the Council Members showed a sympathetic attitude towards the problems of child care, but the subject did evoke some hostility from the late Mr. W. H. Lane of

Penzance. Although the expenditure of the Children's Committee never rose beyond reasonable limits, Mr. Lane aroused some amusement by suggesting at a Council Meeting that it would be cheaper to put deprived children into three-star hotels than to meet their cost in our Children's Homes.

I shall never forget the roar of amusement and applause evoked on a very different occasion when the controversial matter of a dam in West cornwall came up for discussion at a Council Meeting. Every member at a quarterly meeting is given a copy of all the previous Committee Minutes in what was always known as 'the Volume'. The Chairman would then go through 'the volume' page by page, allowing any members who wished to do so to stand up and state the page and paragraph of the item on which he wished to be heard.

By an extraordinary coincidence when the matter of the dam arose, Mr. Lane announced that he wished to speak on page 'H', para 20, this was too much for the Council members who dissolved into laughter.

I was to retire in the spring of 1972 and early that year the ritual of farewell parties and presentations began. I had dreaded this part of leaving and found everyone's kindness most moving.

I think the most painful moment came when I had to empty my desk and found one drawer entirely full of snaps and photos of children which fosterparents and adoptive parents had sent to me over the years. Looking at these I could not fail to realise all I had to lose.

I was glad when the final partings were over, and I had turned the last page of what had been a long and very happy chapter of my life. Of course there was no question of my leaving Cornwall. Much as I loved Gower there were too many ghosts of happier times to attract me back to Wales. I was fortunate in having my mother and sister, Marjorie, to live with me in the Salt Box at Point, the cottage I had found by the water on my arrival in the County. After devoting a lifetime of work for others in the East End of London, Marjorie greatly enjoyed her retirement to the quiet of the Cornish countryside and was an excellent addition to the household. My mother, too, remained remarkably alert and energetic in spite of having reached the 90's.

I still kept in friendly touch with many of the colleagues with whom I had worked for so long in the Children's Department, and was always delighted to have news of boys and girls who had grown up in our care. Nearly twenty years after my retirement, it is still a joy to get letters from some who are now the parents of grown up children. At Christmas, 1991, the wife of one of my Cornish emigrants to Australia sent me news in their Christmas card that their daughter had married and their son had just started at University.

Another girl, Paula, who had been in care when she was four years old, sent me a sheaf of glorious photos of herself, her husband and their two children, and of their idyllic home, which indicated both happiness and prosperity.

I like to think that the success stories outnumber the sad failures, though these can never be forgotten.

Chapter 25
And now....

Now that my main interest in life, Social Work, had come to a halt, I felt free to pursue another, which was that of conservation. For years I had been concerned at the insidious surge of what has been described as 'bungaloid growth' which threatened to destroy the beauty of Restronguet Creek where I live. With the formation of the new District Councils to replace the rural and urban authorities, I decided to stand for election for Carrick District Council, where one of the other two male contenders was a local builder and developer. I thought it high time that women played a part in the world of Local Government, then (as now) still largely a masculine domain.

I enjoyed canvassing in Feock parish and got to know more about it than I had done in all the years I had lived there. I found most people quite friendly and interested, though many remained puzzled about the various functions of the Parish, District and County Councils, and some could not have cared less.

I must confess that I took the election fairly lightly. My canvassing had its amusing moments. I shall not forget the time in Devoran when a woman rushed out of her house as I was passing, clutched me by the arm and said "The women of Devoran are for you". Rightly or wrongly, I succeeded in getting elected and so had my first experience of acting as a Councillor instead of an official in Local Government. The experience was not a happy one. I chose the Housing and Planning Committees on which to serve, but too often found myself in a lonely minority when decisions came to the vote.

The District Council was brand new but the majority of its Councillors had previously served on the now defunct rural or city councils and seemed slow to accept change. I have never been noted for my patience and during the three years that I served on Carrick District council I never really felt at home there, nor that I was adequately representing the people who had elected me. Due largely to my own shortcomings I found myself to be much less successful as a Committee member than when I was employed to do the work.

In spite of making a few excellent friends on Carrick and I hope making no enemies, I did not hesitate to give up my seat when, fresh elections came about after three years. Even so, I was not to be left idle.

The day after my retirement from the County Council I had a telephone call from York to ask me if I would act as the Family Fund's agent in Cornwall. The Family Fund had been set up some years earlier by the Rowntree Trust, in conjunction with the Government which funded it. Its aim was to give extra help to families in Britain who were caring for severely handicapped children. Up to then applications to the Fund for help in Cornwall had been dealt with from Plymouth, but as the work involved increased, it had been decided to appoint an agent in this County.

I gladly accepted this appointment, which exactly suited my long-standing interest in children, and my knowledge of Cornwall. An additional bonus was the good contact I had with the other voluntary and statutory agencies concerned with children in the County.

The Family Fund was centred in York and worked largely through correspondence with its agents all over the country. As soon as a letter asking for help from a family in Cornwall was received by the Fund, a copy would be sent to me with a request to visit the family. Following this I would complete a very full report of its circumstances, the needs of the child and my own recommendation. These often went much further than the family's original request, and might include a holiday for the handicapped child as well as vital equipment to lessen the strain on the hard pressed parents.

There was virtually no cash limit, and after years spent in the tight web of Local Government economies, I found it a great pleasure not to be bound to consider cost as a first priority.

I very much enjoyed the long trips involved in visiting families all over Cornwall, and although the job was unpaid, my travelling costs were met, so that I had no anxieties on that score.

The Family Fund's administrators showed concern and compassion in their work and were a pleasure to deal with. Above all I was deeply impressed by the care and devotion shown to their handicapped children by the parents I met. Some were on call by night and day and I marvelled at their love and patience, particularly with those children who had suffered brain damage and could not speak or respond normally to their parents' affection.

I remember visiting one single girl with a severely mentally handicapped child of seven who demanded total care as he was also incapable of movement. When I asked her if her son could respond in any way to the love she showed him, I was told that he would sometimes clasp her finger if it was placed in his hand. This was all, I could only feel the deepest admiration and humility in the face of such self-sacrifice, and was delighted to give these families every help I could.

I formed a high opinion of the work of the Family Fund which was directed from its Headquarters in York with care and compassion and a minimum of red tape. Although my contact with our Head Office was almost entirely by correspondence and the telephone it was nonetheless warm and friendly. Occasionally the Director, Mrs. Barnes, would come to Cornwall, and on one occasion, (in seven years) I attended a small conference at the Rowntree Head Office in York. It was good to come face to face with staff previously only known by remote control, and I was impressed by the efficient effort and imagination that went into the work.

172

An added bonus was the fact that information on the needs of severely handicapped children culled from reports by the agents of the Family Fund, were passed on to the Government. In this way it was hoped to highlight the special needs of this most vulnerable group when new legislation was considered.

During the seven year stint I did as the Family Fund's agent in Cornwall, I suffered the sad loss of my dear mother shortly before her 98th birthday, and then of my sister, Marjorie, five years later. Both had been of inestimable help to me in my work and in my whole life. I was greatly shattered by their loss, not so much from a fear of living alone, but because our intuitive understanding and love for each other could never be regained.

However, my lucky star did not desert me and within a year I had linked my lot with an old friend and neighbour, John Fox, whose first wife had been a dear friend before her death. The Salt Box had to be stretched a little to accommodate a large man, but that was soon done and we returned there to live happily ever afterwards.

At over 70 I felt it was something of a feat to acquire two stepsons, two granddaughters and even two great grandchildren in place of the vast throng of other people's children with whom I had been concerned for so many years.

Every Christmas brings reminders from the past. Some success stories from the children who have won through, others who sadly seemed doomed to bad luck all their lives. William Blake put it far better than I can when he wrote:-

Every night and every morn

Some to misery are born

Every morn and every night

Some are born to sweet delight....

I can only hope that, in spite of inevitable failures and mistakes, the final account of my happy working years with other people's children will show up on the credit side, and this rather rambling portrayal of them may be of some interest, especially to those still pursuing the elusive goal of being of real social service to those in greatest need. Far too often their efforts receive public notice only when things go wrong. Disasters are given large print and coverage by the media, while work that turns out well goes unreported.

None of us has the wisdom of Solomon, I can only quote my own life long maxim, which is to do one's very best and not to be bowled over if things go wrong.

I myself have been extraordinarily fortunate throughout a long life, and can say with absolute authority that it is better to be born lucky than rich.

Dorothy Watkins

April 1992